MATT BAKER

NEXT LEVEL
LANDLORD

Join the top 5% and
develop HMOs and co-living
spaces where tenants
stay and pay

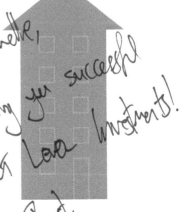

Michelle,
Wishing you successful
Next Level Investments!
Best,
Matt   July 2024

R^ethink

First published in Great Britain in 2021
by Rethink Press (www.rethinkpress.com)

Illustrations have been designed using resources from
Flaticon.com

Contents

Introduction

When I first stumbled into property investing, my only experience of letting was of having been a tenant myself – I had lived in a number of shared situations for years. In 2015, I took a course on how to invest in property without any capital, and it changed my life. I enjoy it and it's been successful beyond my imagining, but it's also given me far more than that.

I have learned to build a business by focusing on the customer, the tenant: the seed of my business. By nurturing that seed, giving it what it needs to flourish and grow, tending to it lovingly and making sure its environment is as ideal as I can make it. I have reaped success when it has borne fruit that sustains my business and family for years to come.

Many people harbour dreams of becoming a successful property investor, developing a property and creating solid cash flow that frees them from the tedium and pressure of a nine-to-five (or longer) job.

You might be someone who has either inherited or saved a considerable sum of money and are anxious to make it work hard for you, so you don't have to continue to work so hard – or at all – for someone else.

You might be a property owner already, perhaps a landlord who wants to expand your holdings, or whose portfolio isn't as profitable as you'd like it to be. You want to find a way to boost your bottom line significantly, using little or no cash or equity of your own.

You might be the owner of a construction company who would like to expand or transition into building assets that you control, building equity where the quality you provide benefits you and your loved ones, instead of those who hire you.

Whether you're sitting on a solid portfolio of assets and equity, or are eager to learn how to get started without waiting to build up a huge nest egg, this book is for you. Together we will explore the ins-and-outs of property investment and development, and how to:

- Deal with houses in multiple occupation (HMOs)

- Identify the ideal property

- Deal with financing, licensing and town councils
- Create a space that tenants clamour to rent
- Market to those tenants
- Ensure solid cash flow and work efficiently

I have been on both sides of the renting equation as a tenant for many years, and a landlord for more than five years. I have gained a lot of experience in letting property, particularly shared accommodation, which has given me valuable perspective and informed our successful 'Tenant First' methodology.

But before this, I had no background in property – I was a musician. I started playing the piano at age five and studied music at Edinburgh University, aiming to work in sound engineering and recording studios. I headed to London, initially sofa-surfing while I joined band after band, doing cover gigs to support myself. But when I factored in the travel, set-up, rehearsal and prep time, I was making far less than minimum wage. After five years, I left London and began a music school which, while growing, just wasn't enough to satisfy me in the long term.

My wife at the time, Alex, urged me to attend a conference that featured talks tailored to small business owners looking to grow. I perked up when Gill Fielding, a well-respected and longstanding property investor and educator, spoke about investing in property without it being full-time or having any seed capital. I had always thought that I would make my money in music, then invest my profits into property as a way of storing wealth; but Gill made a convincing argument to do it the other way around: invest in myself and property first, to allow me the time to invest into creating music on my own terms.

I subsequently did a course with her, then a mentorship, and joined her family of investors. There were so many success stories: buy-to-lets and houses in multiple occupation (HMOs) galore. We took more courses, gained a mentor and began navigating a new path for ourselves.

That's when my life changed. I've never looked back.

What I enjoyed about music was community: being a pianist can be lonely, with few opportunities to join bands, orchestras or ensembles. It was when I began to play with others that I genuinely started to enjoy myself – I got the urge to create great music in partnerships with others. This theme has followed me into my business – and now property – adventure.

Once we chose a target location for our first property, my parents expressed an interest when we discussed our plans. No pressure, I insisted, when I suggested doing it as a family: we were doing it with or without them, I said. They got on board.

After that first year, with two properties under my belt, I approached Niall Scott, who had taken the Fielding Financial course with me and had since developed his own property. I suggested a buy-to-let joint venture. We bought three properties together in quick succession, which marked the official beginning of our partnership, Scott Baker Properties Ltd, in 2017. Our mentors and coaches were a huge part of our success, nudging (sometimes kicking) us forward.

I began sharing with others what was going right and wrong. I was asked to present at a Fielding Financial event, and went on to lead some of their courses. In the meantime, Niall and I set up our own three-pronged business and corresponding brands: Scott Baker Properties, The HMO Platform and a podcast, *Property Jam*.

Scott Baker Properties is our lead development business. It buys, develops and rents HMO and community living ('co-living') projects via investor and joint venture finance. The HMO Platform is our training brand, which provides HMO and co-living workshops and mastermind groups to support landlords with the knowledge and accountability required to get into HMOs and take them to the next level. And *Property Jam* is our no-nonsense podcast, where we talk about all things relating to the human side of property and share stories of our experiential learning.

There is still so much untapped potential in the HMO and co-living market. 'Write it down,' my mentors and coaches urged me. I realised that I could help many more get started in providing needed, quality housing options to those whose lifestyles benefit from shared housing, or people who can't afford to buy.

I could have done with a guidebook myself when I was getting started – so here it is for you.

I first dipped my toe into property in March 2015. Since then, it has been a rollercoaster ride as life can be, both personally and professionally. There was so much I didn't know: relationships broke down, new ones formed, and I am regularly confronted by the reminder that the buck stops with me. Sometimes we crawled uphill or found ourselves hurtling down at breath-taking speed, often being lifted up at the last minute, exhilarated, to further heights.

To that end, this book is an open and honest account of what has and hasn't worked for us. It makes this as smooth as possible a process for you, by sharing the inside perspective from a successful hands-on investor and landlord. I hope it will help you to be well prepared for the inevitable challenges that lie ahead – better than we were. My goal is to help you avoid the same mistakes we made, streamline your path to successful HMO investing, and to become a Next Level Landlord.

You may be wondering if the HMO market is for you. Go to networking events across the country and you might hear: 'The HMO market is dead!' or 'The HMO market is saturated!'

Actually, I agree. The part of the market where most HMOs are has become commoditised: it's all about price now. In fact, it isn't such a bad thing for potential landlords to believe that the HMO market is difficult to crack, because it's true – and will start to put off more potential investors. Landlords are being prodded, poked and squeezed from every direction by government, councils, HM Revenue & Customs, banks, competition in the marketplace and tenants, making executing successful HMOs more challenging. But we have proved it can still work well when you focus on implementing the five Tenant First principles of being a Next Level Landlord.

Despite the pandemic of 2020, the HMO market is evolving and becoming something new, with opportunities for responsible, quality HMO landlords. I'm going to show you how to level up your property portfolio and capitalise on it. This book shares not just the hows of being a Next Level HMO® property investor, but also touches on many of the whys and whos: snippets that highlight what my team and I have gone through to achieve results.

For me it always comes back to building a sense of community, creating something amazing for the benefit of all involved. When this intersects with a great business, the magic happens.

PART ONE
THE FUNDAMENTALS

1

This Business Would Be Great... If It Weren't For The Tenants

I had just come off stage, speaking at a property conference, when I received a frantic call from one of our first HMO tenants. The house he was in was great for 2016: grey feature walls, furniture pack, sitting room and Banksy-inspired artwork chosen by my mum. Because we'd spent a bit more than planned on the property, we chose to self-manage it to boost the bottom line. But against all advice from colleagues, coaches and mentors, I had accepted our first applicants without hesitation or doing full background checks. (It's easy to get carried away in the excitement of populating your first property.)

Two of the tenants had taken a dislike to each other, and things eventually got physical: one had pinned the other down and was repeatedly hitting him. The property was in Warrington and I was in London when I got the call, so there was no way I could get there fast enough to address the issue. I was aware that tensions had been building: that as tenants they were not a good match and shouldn't be sharing a space together. The question was how to deal with it.

The police attended and said that if the victim chose to press charges, the attacker wouldn't be allowed back into the property – and that's what happened. The victim remained resident, while the accused left to stay with a family member (he later agreed to sign a Deed of Surrender and moved out).

Despite the conflict – and to our relief – all of the tenants continued to pay their rent. We refunded a portion of his rent to the tenant who moved out, and relet the property to a new tenant two days later.

TOP TIP

Don't let the excitement of your first property throw caution to the wind. Screen your tenants in advance to avoid headaches later.

Make a start

By no means would this be the only conflict among our tenants. Ignorance is bliss, and if someone had been frank with me at the start about the issues I would encounter on my journey to becoming an HMO landlord and co-living developer, I think I'd have run the other way – but I'm glad I didn't. It's so important to get moving. The most important step you will take along the road to success is your first one.

To be successful, we need a certain amount of fear-lessness – or willingness to assume risk. We have to be willing to make the jump, but with our eyes open.

My goal starting out was to double my portfolio size every year for the first three years. Such rapid growth inevitably brings challenges, but of course with challenges come opportunities to learn. We tend to see the wealthiest and most successful people out there through a rosy filter of apparent overnight success. We aren't aware of what it took, or how long, for them to get where they are. How many played out of tune, off the beat, unsure of the next note to hit, before figuring out the right chords and go on to superstardom?

EDISON: FROM FAILURE TO SUCCESS

The inventor Thomas Edison is arguably one of the best examples of such a success story. He created more than 3,000 light bulb designs, then painstakingly tested more than 6,000 different plants in his quest to determine which would burn the longest and serve as the most suitable filament.[1]

---

1   V Kumar, 'Who invented the lightbulb: The complete truth' (RankRed, 2020), www.rankred.com/who-invented-the-light-bulb, accessed 19 November 2020

This was a man who never gave up, despite failure after failure.

We learn from our mistakes – if we choose to. The concept of failure is a fallacy: nothing more than a learning curve, a winnowing of possible alternatives, the next step on the road to success.

No doubt those of you who are landlords already have your share of horror stories and war wounds, but also your fair share of success stories and positive moments.

We have houses that throw birthday parties for the other tenants and play board games together. And others that you never hear a peep from, because they're so happy to call it their home. That is success!

Learn to love your tenants

I'm sure you will have heard of the Pareto Principle: the 80/20 rule[2] where roughly 80% of the effects come from 20% of the causes. For Next Level HMOs, it is no longer 80:20, it's 95:5. If you focus your attention on creating a co-living portfolio in the top 5% of all the shared properties in your areas, you will have a much easier life. This is the top 5% in design, space and service (more on this in Chapter 2).

---

2   R Koch, *The 80/20 Principle: The secret to achieving more with less*, 3rd
     edition (Broadway Business, 1999)

Tenants are the lifeblood of our business, so if we spend the necessary time to get this bit right, we can learn to love our tenants. And we must: they pay for our mortgages, cars and holidays, and help us ensure financial security for the future.

The next time you find yourself moaning or complaining about something a tenant just did, remember the mantra: 'Love your tenants,' as they're providing your income now and in the future.

2
Next Level HMOs

As we saw in the Introduction, anything commoditised has low profitability.

APPLE: BANISHING THE BEIGE

In the late 1990s, computers had become beige boxes while the profit margins had dropped to single digits, as Compaq, Hewlett Packard and Dell all competed.

Then Steve Jobs shows up in the marketplace with a product that's anything but: colourful, see-through boxes – completely different, exciting-looking computers. The profit margins on Apple computers jumped to more than 25%,[3] with a strategy all about profitability, not market share.

---

3   D Knight, 'Apple's 1999 financials' (Low End Mac, 1999), https://lowendmac.com/1999/apples-1999-financials, accessed 19 November 2020

> You could buy any number of beige boxes, but there
> was only one iMac.

In this book we're going to explore what the property equivalent would look like: a colourful, creative, interesting HMO. That's the one that's going to make the profit when tenants are out there looking at properties to live in, are excited to move into and for which they're willing to pay more.

Creating attractive properties

As we saw in Chapter 1, follow the 95:5 rule and become the top 5% – the only one doing what you do in your area (Figure 2.1). As Apple dropped the word 'computer' from what it sells, drop the ordinary from yours: it's no longer an HMO, but a 'shared-living community' or 'co-living experience'. No longer a room to let, but a home in which to enjoy months and years of life.

Plenty of people out there will try to convince you that to be a successful landlord, you should create a soulless, empty property devoid of all personality. But the truth of that is ending up with constantly rotating tenants: your life will become increasingly taken up by the mundane problems of running a poorly performing portfolio.

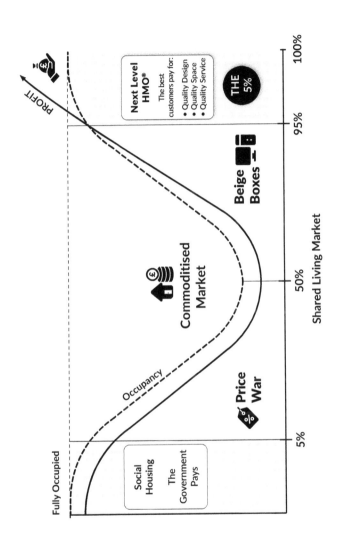

PROFIT

Fully Occupied

Social
Housing

The
Government
Pays

Price
War

Occupancy

Commoditised
Market

Beige
Boxes

Next Level
HMO®

The best
customers pay for:
• Quality Design
• Quality Space
• Quality Service

THE
5%

5%   50%   95%   100%

Shared Living Market

Figure 2.1: Be the 5%

I expect you to question this assumption and logic, to say there's no money in doing the basic, boring stuff. But read on.

What is an HMO?

This is a national, technical definition in the Housing Act 2004, which is, in summary: 'An entire house or flat, which is let to three or more tenants who are not from one household, for example, a family, and who share a kitchen, bathroom or toilet'.[4]

An HMO is defined by the Government, so it certainly can be used to describe most types of shared accommodation.

How do you perceive a typical HMO, what does it conjure up in your mind? Do you see it, as some do, as a derogatory word to describe a slum? Do you see the rinse-and-repeat beige box, or an insightful way to provide quality accommodation to those who cannot afford independent housing?

When we saw the term 'HMO' being used to describe lots of different types of properties – the good, the bad and the downright ugly – we coined the term 'Next Level HMO®', which we registered to distinguish us

---

4   This is covered in more detail in Sections 254–7 of the Housing Act 2004: www.legislation.gov.uk/ukpga/2004/34/section/254.

from the other, arguably lesser standard of HMOs out there.

This distinction is about more than just design; it's about what makes a property desirable to a tenant while remaining profitable for us. It means taking our whole business concept to a new level.

The Next Level HMO®

There are six facets to the Next Level HMO®, covering the benefits to both investor and tenant.

The Next Level HMO®…

- **Offers good return on investment.** The Next Level HMO® frees up equity by adding value to the property, while maintaining high cash flow.

- **Benefits from economies of scale.** One way we get a high return and cash flow is to target slightly larger properties where we can design more income-producing rooms in a building. Why? Because running costs don't increase proportionally with an increase in the number of rooms. For example, to run a six-bed HMO doesn't cost all that much less than running an eight-bed HMO, and because the eight-bed property generates more income, it leaves more cash in your pocket at the end of each month.

- **Has achieved planning permission.** This happens either as a small HMO in an area with a relevant Article 4 directive,[5] or with seven or more occupants. Why? Because planning permission can dramatically increase the value of a property.

- **Is a converted building.** The Next Level HMO® is often an old, underused commercial building converted into a cluster of flats. For example, by taking an old office block and dividing it up to create seven three-bed flats, it can be designed as shared rental accommodation for twenty-one people.

- **Is a design-led property.** Tenants need to love the place in which they live. There's no point in creating a product, no matter how wonderful, if there is no target market. Before you begin, the most important task is to research your end user and create a product that meets their needs. For example, while some people might not mind or even enjoy living with seven other individuals, others may vastly prefer to live with just two or three other people.

- **Is a service-led property.** Giving your customer – your tenant – their best experience at whatever stage of life they are, ensures that they stay for a long time and rave about you as a landlord.

---

5   An Article 4 directive removes your permitted development right to convert a family home to an HMO with up to six individuals. See Chapter 5 for more information.

Wouldn't it be great if your business could start to sustain itself just from word of mouth?

However you get there, the point is the same: create a product that's better designed, and a service head and shoulders above its competitors. Your property will be more profitable and much more valuable. It's highly likely that by focusing on these points, the property has now become a co-living property.

3
What Is Co-living?

'Community living' is a buzzword that has become popular relatively recently but has been around for a long time. Like the term 'HMO', it means different things to different people; but the popular association leans towards the image of a group of people living harmoniously in a shared community.

Technically, the difference between an HMO and co-living is the 'co' bit: the environment and space to commune with others. We believe that the community aspect of a property needs to be designed from day one into the fabric of the building, but also needs to be nurtured when people occupy it. As the operators of the building, you have a vested interest in the happiness of your tenants – because if they're happy, they will stay and pay.

CO-LIVING: A POTTED HISTORY

Co-living is a way of life dating back to the Stone Age. Indigenous peoples typically constructed dwellings to house multiple families and often livestock, sharing facilities, farming and eating together. We have more modern examples of this in the UK, including purpose-built tenements in Scotland in the 1700s onwards. These properties were large, multi-occupancy buildings housing many families, although they gained a bad name because of overcrowding. Ironically, these Scottish tenements are now highly sought after because of their size, high ceilings, large windows and prime locations.

In the twentieth century, community became paramount during the two world wars. In 1933–34, the architect Wells Coates OBE designed and constructed the Isokon Building (also called the Lawn Road Flats) in Hampstead, north-west London. The building was an attempt to create a sense of co-living with both private space and a shared kitchen, later converted into a cafe bar.

The project also introduced the idea of services for the community as part of the living experience, including shoe cleaning, laundry, bed-making and food delivered by a dumb waiter in the spine of the building. It was a famous landmark in its time, and residents included the writer, Agatha Christie. It is now occupied as flats and has been Grade I listed since 1974.

Moving into the twenty-first century, the evolution of larger co-living developments appears to have grown in the smaller HMO and shared-living world. For example, in Silicon Valley around the early 2000s, many tech workers in start-ups shared what became known as 'hacker houses', where people lived and worked together under one roof. The houses were not just HMOs in the traditional sense, but shared with a community. Another example of this type of community-based development is student blocks and halls of residence. These instil community because of the tenants' common goals and stage of life. As developers started to see the business opportunity and social opportunity, they turned to larger cities, namely New York and London, with Berlin following closely behind.

HMOs versus co-living

What's the difference today between HMOs and co-living? An HMO is a technical definition of a property featuring three or more unrelated individuals who share some facilities. Think of co-living as an HMO-plus: a lifestyle that comes from community – the tenants' living environment. It's the existence of social spaces to come together, eat and enjoy entertainment with others. There is also enough space for people to live and work. Work from home opportunities are becoming increasingly normal in this day and age of the gig economy, especially in the post-Covid-19 world.

Why is this a popular concept with tenants?

- A lack of suitable affordable housing, particularly for young adults

- Stagnant wages and booming property prices translate to the inability to save sufficient deposits or qualify for sizeable financing, despite historically low interest rates

- A growing interest in non-committal lifestyles, where people prefer not to be tied down to a long contract (much like a no-frills gym membership), or accumulate a lot of furnishings and belongings

- An increase in feelings of loneliness, isolation and depression

These HMO markets in the UK are now dominated by a few large players. We smaller HMO landlords generally manage five to ten people per property, while larger operators manage 200+ in some of their buildings.

At the beginning of 2020, we visited the offices of one of these larger providers, The Collective, to find out how they view HMOs, co-living and the marketplace, and to learn more about their strategy.

THE COLLECTIVE'S STRATEGY

Solicit feedback from tenants (or 'members', as they're called) – tenants are the best source for learning what is and isn't working, so you can do something about the latter; a good feedback loop to you as landlord is vital.

Engage with the local community outside the development – when we understand how to manage an HMO well, it can benefit the community.

Engage with local councils – large schemes require planning permission and licensing among other regulatory issues, so having a good relationship with the council is important. It benefits us to educate them on what a good co-living development should look like, and how it should and would be managed.

Add value – the service layer attached to co-living projects is important, from cleaning communal spaces to organised events and entertainment, both small and large.

When you magnify an idea, like taking HMOs to a large scale, you magnify everything – not just the profits, but the problems too. In addition, some would argue that scale can potentially negatively impact the co-living customer experience. Is it better to be a big fish in a small pond or a tiny fish struggling to find their school in the ocean? Both large and small scale have their challenges, but regardless, tenant well-being contributes to overall community well-being, and as landlords and operators, it is our moral and ethical imperative to take our tenants' quality of life seriously.

It's not just the right thing to do; it also makes sense from a business perspective, because as we've already seen, happy tenants are often long-term tenants. If we create a contented community for them, they'll spread the word.

How do we begin to go about this? By using the 'Tenant First' methodology.

4
The Tenant First Method

For any business to be successful, it has to meet a need. As we've identified, the focus needs to be on the customer first: what they're looking for, and how you can meet their needs. Identify the problems, devise a solution, then create your business around that solution.

The problem with housing

In property, the problem for customers is clear: a large shortage of housing nationwide. There is a growing population, but not enough places to house people or pace of building to match the growth. The most recent figures show a demand for 1.2 million additional homes in 2020, predicted to increase over the next 15 years to another 4 million homes.[6]

The Government reports that in the UK over the last five years, we have built or converted properties as follows (Table 4.1).

Table 4.1: *Property construction and conversion in the UK, 2014–19*[7]

Calendar year	New-build completions	Total net additional dwellings	Total through conversion
2014–15	140,760	171,000	30,240
2015–16	147,730	190,000	42,270
2016–17	156,140	217,000	60,860
2017–18	164,510	222,000	57,490
2018–19	165,160	241,000	75,840

The total number of additional dwellings is increasing, but the conversion realm is increasing at a far greater rate, which shows that small landlords and developers are having a positive impact. Despite this higher rate of increase, it still isn't sufficient to meet the need for another 4 million housing units in 15 years.

---

6   *BBC Briefing: Housing* (BBC, 2020), http://news.files.bbci.co.uk/ include/newsspec/pdfs/bbc-briefing-housing-newsspec-26534.pdf, accessed 19 November 2020

7   *House Building: New build dwellings, England, September quarter, 2019* (Ministry of Housing, Communities & Local Government, 2020), www.gov.uk/government/statistics/house-building-new-build-dwellings-england-july-to-september-2019, accessed 19 November 2020

THE TENANT FIRST METHOD

Are we likely to continue to build or convert at this rate? Are there enough contractors and materials? No wonder shared accommodation is widely needed in the UK.

Who is shared living for?

There are so many different sources of tenants that we must be specific about what we are supplying as a product, and to whom:

- Single people without partners or roommates

- Couples that can't afford their own flat to buy or rent

- Younger generations who don't yet command the salaries to get their first home

- Younger generations who don't want the commitment of a home or dealing with bills – who like the idea of all-inclusive properties

- Separated people in midlife who may have children living with their former partner

- Older generations who are downsizing and want a sense of community

- Temporary workers who have a home somewhere else, but need a pied-à-terre from Monday to Friday

- University students who live in the area for nine to twelve months of the year

What is the demand in the area where we are looking to invest? Having identified that, we can supply the answer.

The five principles of a Next Level Landlord

Everything begins with the tenant, which is why Niall and I formulated Tenant First as the way to create successful Next Level HMOs and become a Next Level Landlord. Throughout this book we will refer to the five principles of this method (Figure 4.1).

If you follow these in the correct order, you can massively increase the chances of your properties being full and lasting the test of time, giving you great income and return on your cash.

Focus

Identify your why and how:

- Understand the basics
- Have a business plan
- Create brand value and your own design blueprint

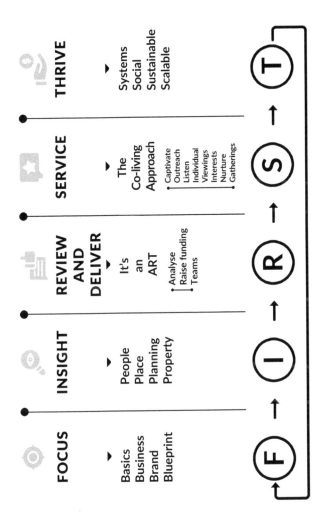

Figure 4.1: The Tenant First method

FOCUS
- Basics
- Business
- Brand
- Blueprint

INSIGHT
- People
- Place
- Planning
- Property

REVIEW AND DELIVER
- It's an ART
  - Analyse
  - Raise funding
  - Teams

SERVICE
- The Co-living Approach
  - Captivate
  - Outreach
  - Listen
  - Individual
  - Viewings
  - Interests
  - Nurture
  - Gatherings

THRIVE
- Systems
- Social
- Sustainable
- Scalable

F → I → R → S → T

Insight

Know the business like the back of your hand:

- The people who are your customers
- The place where you will invest
- The planning rules that give you uplift in value
- The properties and how to find them effectively

Review and deliver

This truly is an artform, because it's where the money is made:

- Analyse deals – know your numbers
- Raise finance – leverage finance options
- Teams – build the best people around you to deliver

Service

Concentrate on great service:

- Use the Co-living Approach to improve your quality of tenant
- Know how to get and keep the best tenants

Thrive

Get the best out of your operation:

- Use systems to get your time back
- Take a sustainable approach to projects
- Leverage social media and profile-raising to raise finance and form partnerships
- Scale the business in a measured way

Put the tenant at the heart of all your decision-making, *not* the property or deal.

PART TWO
FOCUS

5
Focus On The Basics

Before we detail how to execute this strategy, there is some essential information to focus on first.

If you're already an HMO landlord, most of what is in this chapter should be familiar, but keep reading! If you are new to HMOs, please pay close attention to the definitions, rules and regulations set out. Quite a lot of property professionals don't always grasp the rules.

Due to differing remits, also don't be surprised if different departments within the council give different answers to the same question surrounding HMOs. This is especially the case concerning licensing, planning and building regulations. Some councils will be helpful while others will not, and some will immediately put up roadblocks when you mention you intend to create an HMO. Knowing how to work with councils and get them on side will make your investing career a lot easier.

The HMO

We've examined the technical definition of an HMO in Chapter 2. Across the whole of the UK, HMOs are defined as three or more individuals from more than one family unit who live together with separate bedrooms and shared common areas.

Let's look at a few examples (see figure 5.1):

- Two people living together as roommates does not constitute an HMO.

- Three people living together as roommates does constitute an HMO.

- Two couples (four individuals) living together does constitute an HMO, because it is more than three people from two households.

The precise number of individuals sharing a property does not dictate whether an entity is an HMO or not. For example, you could have a family of ten, which would not be an HMO.

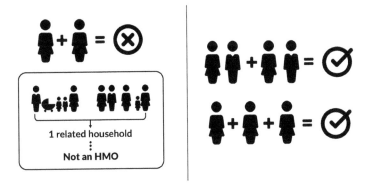

Figure 5.1: Definition of HMO (people)

I suspect the rationale behind this is that, in the case of fire, a family would ensure all of its members exit the building, knowing who has and has not left. Conversely, independent roommates who live separate lives won't necessarily know the others' comings and goings. Moreover, they may not feel responsible for helping others escape (although one would hope that most people would).

The key number to remember here is three. A lot of people mistakenly think that HMOs start at either five or six people, the result of crossed wires between licensing and planning rules.

HMO licensing

There are two main types:

- Mandatory licensing – the national licensing scheme issued by the Government
- Additional licensing – the local level of licence that councils can opt to bring in

A third, selective licensing, is a local licence that councils can bring in to apply to all rental properties in a selected area. (HMOs are caught within that, but the criteria for getting this more general licence are simpler than that of an HMO licence.)

Mandatory licensing

Beginning in October 2018, mandatory licensing governs any property which has **five** or more unrelated people. To obtain the necessary licence, you must apply as soon as the fifth person or household is installed. Because councils can take considerable time to address licence applications, most will allow you to operate while the application is going through.

Additional licensing

This type of licensing has been brought in by certain councils which are more concerned about the standards of HMOs sited in their town. They are also likely to be more on top of their application and assessment process, because it increases the number of licensable HMOs.

By reducing the council's threshold for the number of unrelated occupants in a property from five to four, or even three, more properties are required to be licensed. If the council has an additional licensing scheme for three or more unconnected people, every single HMO would require a licence.

To obtain a licence, complete your local council's application form, either online or by hand. It is a lengthy form that requires floor plans of the property, and all the measurements to prove room sizes. If you use a management agent, there are sections they must complete as well.

Each council has a set of standards that you need to comply with; the most important ones are the governing national minimum room sizes.[8] If you are renting to adults, the minimum bedroom sizes at a national level are:

- Single-occupancy: 6.51 m^2
- Double-occupancy: 10.22 m^2

These minimum sizes include built-in wardrobes, but not:

8   See the amendment to Schedule 4 of the Housing Act 2004: www.legislation.gov.uk/uksi/2018/616/regulation/2/made.

- En-suite bathrooms (deemed to be washing facilities)

- Any floor area with less than 1.5 m of ceiling height

- Any space deemed unusable corridor

- Chimney breasts

To get your licence, you must be deemed a fit and proper person – ie, you must not have certain unspent criminal convictions or have contravened laws relating to housing. The licence price may exceed £1,000, but it will last you five years. For a six-bed HMO, that is less than £3 per month per tenant.

TOP TIP

Get the licence in your name, not your agent's. If you change agents, you will need to apply and pay again. We have changed agents before, and were grateful we avoided this extra cost by not licensing in their name.

Residential property use classes

In the UK, you need planning permission to create an HMO. HMOs have their own use class, and buildings are categorised in the UK by how a property can be used. The change of use of any building or piece of land also requires planning permission.

There are mechanisms in place that allow change of use without asking first: permitted development rights. We will explore in more detail in Chapter 10 how to use planning permission and permitted development rights to piece together your own Next Level HMO® strategy; but for now, let's look at the basic definitions you need to know.

Residential property is deemed Class C, of which there are four sub-classes: C1 to C4. They are defined by the Town and Country Planning (Use Classes) Order 1987 (as amended). The 2010 amendment assigned HMOs their own use class: C4.

C3 dwellings are basic residential dwelling houses occupied by one or two households. Once a third household is added, the building is deemed an HMO, changing the classification use from a C3 dwelling house to a C4 HMO. The C4 use class allows for three to six unconnected households at any given time. If occupancy drops to two or one, it becomes C3 again by default.

Article 4 directions

An Article 4 direction enables the Secretary of State or the local planning authority to withdraw specified permitted development rights across a defined area.[9]

---

9   'When is permission required?' (Ministry of Housing, Communities & Local Government, 2014, updated 2020), www.gov.uk/guidance/when-is-permission-required, accessed 19 November 2020

What this in effect means is that any permitted development right (not just those allowing small HMOs) can be removed to protect against certain types of development in those defined areas. A conservation area is the most recognisable use of Article 4 directions nationwide. Change of use from C3 to C4 is a permitted development right (Class L) granted by the Government: in most of the country you can switch back and forth without any issues. But if a council brings in an Article 4 direction, that prohibits change of use from C3 to C4 without first obtaining full planning permission. This doesn't mean that it won't be granted, but it is harder to get.

Always verify whether your target area is governed by an Article 4 directive before you change a C3 dwelling to a C4 HMO. (We like Article 4 areas; the reasons for this will become clearer as you read on.)

Note that Article 4 directions can be used to stop *any* permitted development right, not simply HMOs, so you must determine the reason for it, if it exists. For example, a conservation area would be put in place using an Article 4 direction. Check with the council to determine what any Article 4 direction governs.

Sui generis

Planning for HMOs may involve *sui generis*, a Latin term meaning 'in a class of its own'. Once the Government had classed the majority of property types in the UK, some were judged not to require a use class of their own. For example, casinos, launderettes and large HMOs of seven or more unconnected people fall outside of the use class schedule and are *sui generis*.[10]

When we apply for planning permission for seven, eight or nine distinct tenants, we are applying for *sui generis*. That is a full planning application every time, and to get it approved, it's important to understand the planning policies in the respective area.

Like the Article 4 direction, it doesn't mean that planning won't be approved, as long as you follow the rules and play the game. In fact, in some areas it's quite easy to get planning for *sui generis* HMOs, because if the council doesn't have a policy, it's harder to find reasons to refuse.

In summary, when it comes to HMO planning, how many people you intend to have living in the property is key. You can have an eight-bedroom property which only has six people living in it, and you haven't broken planning rules. You can create the space and do the works without full planning in place because it only contains the maximum six independent tenants. But as soon as you add a seventh, you have technically breached planning regulations.

---

10 'Use classes' (Planning Portal, 2020), www.planningportal.co.uk/info/200130/common_projects/9/change_of_use, accessed 19 November 2020

Our definition of HMO

Back in Chapter 2 on HMO basics, we asked: 'What is an HMO?'

Most importantly, an HMO is a home for your tenant. Somewhere safe and secure where they can put all their stuff; a place where they can get home at the end of the day and cook, have social space to meet other people, chill out and sleep.

In terms of how we define an HMO, social space is important because some HMOs don't provide any socialising space, while others do. Some are designed for the tenant to have their own space, while in others you can't even swing a cat!

What kind of landlord are you looking to be? What kind of space do you want to create? The Next Level HMO® strategy helps you to decide, and if you choose to create these homes, to become a Next Level Landlord with a conscience.

6
Focus On The Business

Now is an important time to examine your reasons for learning about HMOs. Your real reasons: the primary ones. Your *why* is the first and arguably most vital thing to establish before continuing. It's your starting point to running a successful business.

Your initial answer as to why you're reading this book might be 'to learn about HMO planning permission' or 'to understand commercial valuations'. Believe me, I know this technical stuff can be interesting – I live it!

But why do you want to know it? What is your purpose in wanting to do an HMO, let alone a Next Level HMO®?

Defining your mission, vision and values

If you haven't done so already, take some time to answer these questions:

- What is your mission?

- What is your vision?

- What are your values?

You may have a vague idea, but is it written down and fully defined? If it is, great! You're steps ahead of most. Still, it doesn't hurt to revisit, to rethink and refine the possibilities.

If you haven't yet defined your mission, vision and values, let's get started. This chapter will create the seeds from which your entire business plan can grow.

Mission

Your mission encapsulates why your business exists – or will exist. Let's look at an example:

- **Your focus:** To provide affordable housing

- **For whom:** Those who can't afford to buy or rent their own home

- **Your specific business location (if one):** Brighton

- **Mission:** We provide affordable housing solutions in Brighton to those with limited resources

Now, this example is broad and not terribly distinctive. Think about what makes you stand out. At Scott Baker Properties, we offer Next Level HMOs – it makes us stand out in the marketplace as a developer.

Your first assignment is to give some serious thought to the answer to these questions for your specific business, and write them down. It's OK if your mission, vision and values change over time, so long as you keep track of them by writing them down and updating them. If you're new to property, and this is your first property book, you may not know the answers today – but we encourage you to still have a go.

Some rules for creating a mission statement:

- Be clear and to the point
- Avoid complicated language and jargon
- Make it easily explainable to others
- Make it unique to you

SCOTT BAKER PROPERTIES: OUR MISSION

At Scott Baker Properties we include our social conscience as developers and work with social housing and supported living, which further sets us apart from many investors and developers. Here's our mission statement as an example.

We aspire to be a leader in the UK in providing high-quality shared accommodation and co-living spaces.

We help those who need it most by providing social, supported and emergency LGBT+ friendly housing.

We are determined to provide five-star service for our investors, always acting with honesty and integrity, reliability in performance and communications, and creating a sense of security.

The mission of our training company, The HMO Platform, is to support 100 landlords every year in taking their business to the next level by becoming Next Level Landlords. Because we believe in this so strongly, we created a model, 'Keys to Continued Growth', to illustrate what we aim to achieve – not just in our HMO training, but in every aspect of our business (Figure 6.1).

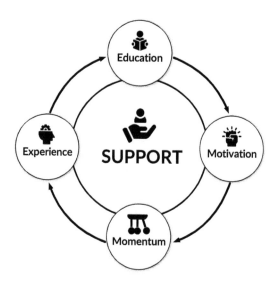

Figure 6.1: Keys to continued growth

We all start by learning, which motivates us to get going, which in turn creates momentum. This leads to the experience of what you have done, which educates you further, and so the cycle perpetuates itself. At the centre of all of this is support.

TOP TIP

Visually displaying your mission adds power to it.

Vision

Where do you see yourself in five years' time? Having a vision is about deciding where you want to go, and mapping out how to get there. There are many ways to do this, including vision boards, statements and stories.

There is a theory that most people overestimate what they can accomplish in a year, but significantly underestimate what they can accomplish in five years. If you had said to me that four years after buying my first property, I would have a portfolio worth almost £5 million, I would flat out not have believed you. I would have believed it were possible for others because I've seen others do it, but not for me. But that is what happened. That has taught me to think bigger and stop underestimating myself.

I created a vision board a few years ago which has things on it beginning to come true. Now, it definitely needs updating. My coaches encouraged me to review my five-year vision, so I do this twice a year to make sure it remains relevant and that I'm still on track.

CREATING A VISION

My vision is a ten-minute recording. I began by brainstorming ideas of what I wanted: a house, car, relationships, lifestyle, health, holidays, etc.

Next, I envisioned an important day in the future and wrote down everything I could think of to describe that day: how and where I woke up; what and who was around me – the sights, smells, sounds.

The more vivid your vision, the more power it has. It comprises both personal and business, because as an entrepreneur the two are entwined.

If you want to create a vision to share with your team and the wider world, you can do that too; perhaps it's a video or photo montage. The ideas are endless, but the goal is the same: put your vision down. Don't just have it in your head, as that's too vague, too ephemeral.

You want to create something concrete that you can look at or listen to regularly. Only then will you see the changes start to happen that move you towards your vision.

TOP TIP

Remember: you are an entrepreneur and business owner when you go into HMOs. If you don't believe that, you're selling yourself short. You can cover this in your vision.

Values

What are your values? To some, values might include honesty and integrity; to others, one's family, friends or business. It's about what's most important to you. Have you ever taken the time to identify what yours are?

Ask yourself: what do I want to be remembered for? The way I suggest you have a go is to write your own obituary.

A NOBEL LEGACY

Alfred Nobel, inventor, engineer and chemist, was a wealthy self-made man who, among other things, invented dynamite. In 1888, on the death of his brother Ludvig, the story goes that Nobel was taken aback to see his own obituary mistakenly printed in a French newspaper, which had confused his brother's death with his own.

It read: 'The merchant of death is dead', going on to identify him as, 'Dr Alfred Nobel, who became rich by finding ways to kill more people faster than ever before.'[11]

---

11 C Schultz, 'Blame sloppy journalism for the Nobel Prizes' (*Smith-sonian Magazine*, 2013), www.smithsonianmag.com/smart-news/blame-sloppy-journalism-for-the-nobel-prizes-1172688, accessed 19 November 2020

Appalled, Nobel realised he wanted a far better legacy. He posthumously donated his fortune to found the Nobel Prize, designed to recognise those individuals judged to have made the greatest annual contribution to humankind in subjects that interested him: physics, chemistry, medicine, literature and peace.

And that is what Nobel is remembered for today, not for his advances in the use of explosives.

If you were to die tomorrow, what would people say about you? What do you want to be known for? Do your actions reflect how you would like to be remembered?

Examples of our company values include:

- Build Community – everything we do is centred around bringing people together.

- Inspire Greatness – everything we do should inspire others to take action towards their own success.

- Be the Best You – bring the right energy to yourself and to your business every day to ensure your own success.

Strategy

Once defined, your mission, vision and values form the backbone of your business strategy and goals. To create the output defined in your mission, what is your input?

Let's look at an example. For income-related goals, what is the desired monthly rent roll, and how many deals do you need to hit this? (We would assume a bare minimum of £150 profit per room, eg if you are looking for £15,000 profit per month, you will need 100 rooms.)

For capital-related goals, what is the desired uplift in equity or capital gain? How many deals do you need to hit this? (We would assume a minimum of 10% uplift per project.)

Say you're looking for £1 million in equity, you need to be doing deals totalling an end value (Gross Development Value, GDV) of £10 million.

This high-level approach will help you to narrow down what you need to do.

7
Your Brand And Blueprint

Now you've established and recorded your mission, vision and values, how can you distinguish yourself from others? What is your unique selling point: the one thing that will make someone remember you or care about your business?

When I speak, I often refer to myself as 'the piano-playing property investor'. How many other property investors have you heard of who describe themselves like that?

Branding

Try this exercise. Write your name in the middle of a piece of paper. Not your business name, but your own name, because your business is essentially you. Around your name, jot down what you do for:

- Work

- Play

- Hobbies

- Leisure time with family or friends

- Travel

- Music

- Sport

- Food

– whatever you can think of that captures who you are. Keep going until you find a theme that you can latch on to, then ask yourself:

- What makes me or my business different?

- What makes me stand out from the rest?

- Why would someone be drawn to me?

- What would make someone care about me?

- What do I not want to be known for?

- Who do I admire for doing strategy well?

- Who do I not want to be linked to?

Once you can answer these questions, you have a great foundation on which to build your property business. From there, do a Strengths–Weaknesses–Opportunities–Threats (SWOT) analysis for your brand:

- What are my and my team's strengths?
- What are my and my team's weaknesses?
- What opportunities are there for me?
- What threats could prevent me from success?

This information will give you personal insight into what you want your brand to be. It can be relayed to a designer to work up the basic brand assets that you need:

- Logo
- Website
- Brochure

When creating these assets, ask yourself the following questions:

- Are they necessary?
- Do I actually need to project an image to anyone?
- Who are these for: potential tenants, investors or other developers?

THE IMPORTANCE OF BRAND VISIBILITY

When Scott Baker Properties started, we didn't have a logo, website or any good-looking information that we could share with people. We had Microsoft PowerPoint and Word and a desire to present information, but not the branding clout that adds so much value.

This was highlighted when we were in discussions with a couple who were looking to invest into the business. They were keen until they couldn't find an online presence for us. In our eyes, whether we had a website or not, we offered exactly the same service – an asset-backed investment – but the lack of a website was our downfall.

We now have one that we are proud of, having engaged the right professionals to deliver it.

Most developers are rubbish at understanding the value of having a brand, and those that do are rubbish at implementing it. This is one way to distinguish yourself from the crowd and make a business that is truly and recognisably yours.

Your blueprint

Your blueprint is how you apply your brand to your portfolio. The easiest way to understand this is in the design of the properties: from the colours of the windows to the shape of the bedhead.

But it can also affect the service that you offer, which we will focus on when we look at the Service principle in Part 5. When creating your Next Level HMO®, as with all elements of Tenant First, we always start with the end in mind in the development process. We focus on the end user and design the product that suits our marketplace, from space standards and amenities to ensuring compliance with all of the licensing and planning legislation.

TOP TIP

It's likely you'll be using a large team to create your end product, so everyone must be on the same page and communicate well with each other. A blueprint is essential to understand this before making a start.

One way to create a blueprint is through a mood board. Register for a Pinterest account, then start to pin images of what you do and don't like.

Place everything you source online or have pictures of, including wall colours, flooring, unit colours (of kitchens and bathrooms) on paper, or use Canva. com. Cast your eye across all of it for tonal harmony, to ensure it's not too dark or light but somewhere in-between. Note in particular the floor, wall and units, because these colours tend to dominate.

Design for your tenants

When designing your blueprint, focus on the tenant. Bedrooms should be peaceful, tranquil and private: a place where it's easy to sleep, retreat and relax. Lighting might be dimmed, beds decorated with attractive throws and large pillows.

In the kitchen and communal spaces, you want to create not just functionality but a sense of community: inclusion, playfulness, relaxation, perhaps creativity. Wall prints, plants (fresh herbs are a nice touch), sofa throws, a stack of board or card games – whatever creates a sense of home.

As responsible and ethical developers, the well-being of our tenants must be at the forefront of our minds – from design through to implementation, furnishing and management. When creating your own blueprint, apply these tips for your residents' overall well-being.

Lighter colours on the walls enhance and reflect lighting. Dark colours which absorb light may look dramatic and elegant at first glance, such as in a hotel; but for long stays they can feel oppressive, even claustrophobic.

Colour can make a space feel bigger, smaller or change the mood of the environment. For smaller rooms, limit bold, dark or bright colours to furnishings, as opposed to walls. For larger rooms, using bolder colours or patterns is tempting as there is more space to play with, but too much can narrow the feel of a space.

Cast your eye across the room as a whole: does it feel balanced? Is there a place that draws your eye more than anywhere else – and if so, why? Can you either tone down that space, or perhaps add two other spaces in the room to balance it?

Curtains are ideal to incorporate pattern, form and colour in a space without attracting too much attention, or making the room appear unbalanced.

Bring the outside in with plants, natural fibres, etc. Even artificial plants introduce nature and trick the brain into feeling better.

High ceilings and regular-shaped rooms, with 90-degree corners create a sense of space (the more angles, the smaller a space feels). Rooms shouldn't be so oversized as to result in unused space – just enough that the tenant doesn't feel cramped.

Staging your property

Your blueprint should result in well-styled marketing assets at the end: photos, videos, tours, etc. This means either styling rooms yourself (eg thumbing through home decorating magazines and websites for inspiration) or using an interior designer to stage them for photographing. Securing a photographer with experience in staging properties can help too. The idea is to draw tenants to want to live in your space.

All of the following props can be reused across the properties you develop:

- Bedrooms – use cosy, soft furnishings in a variety of textures. Add a bedside table with a lamp lit, perhaps a book placed alongside.

- Kitchens – lay the table in a welcoming style, with glasses and perhaps a bottle of wine alongside, accompanied by food – a basket of bread or fruit will do.

- Living room – dress the space with plants, prints and candles, bowls, blankets and cushions.

Your rooms are your shop window, helping tenants to decide whether they can envision living contentedly in your property – it's important to make those spaces inviting.

PART THREE
INSIGHT

8
Insight Into Place

If you're reading this book hoping to discover the golden nugget that shows you which town will be the next HMO hotspot, prepare to be disappointed. The goal is to learn how to *identify* a hotspot, rather than simply following someone else. Lazy investors generally get back what they put in: a lazy return. If you're willing to put in a bit more legwork, you'll have the knowledge to generate greater returns.

As my first mentor in property, Gill Fielding, taught me, where to invest is all about the demand for your product, and a set of circumstances that make the investment viable at a point in time. This is especially true with HMOs, where there are many variables that need pinpointing to calculate whether an area works (Figure 8.1).

Figure 8.1: The DNA of a Next Level HMO® - demand

The first of these variables is demand:

- Is there sufficient and growing demand for your product, the HMO you intend to create?

- Who is your tenant?

Whenever we set up a new business, we want to consider who and where our customer is. In a geocentric business such as providing living accommodation, location is the key factor. But how do we determine what constitutes a good one?

The best locations are not just where a lot of people *want* our service, but where there is a growing number of people who *need* it. Some investors prefer to buy existing HMOs where cash flow is already established: this is a safer way to identify demand, based on existing and historical tenants. Another positive is that by not adding to the HMO supply, you don't need to find new, additional tenants – but you will pay a premium for that property, because everything is in place and ready to go.

Some investors create new HMOs and attempt to uplift the value. This can work well, but a lot of research needs to be done first to understand who and where these new tenants are. When it goes well, demand is fulfilled; when it doesn't, we hear complaints about the HMO market. As mentioned previously, many think that HMOs don't work anymore, that the market for them is saturated. There is some truth to that for certain types of HMOs in certain areas, targeting certain types of tenants; but for other areas and other types of tenants, there is still huge demand for rooms and not enough available.

Where to start?

Three fundamentals are needed to establish a potential location:

1. Healthy population size

2. Strong employment options

3. Great local amenity (Figure 8.2)

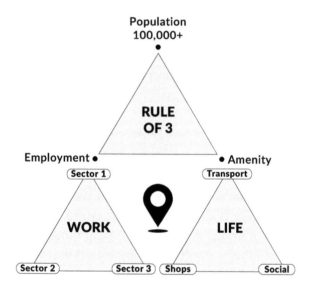

*Figure 8.2: The fundamentals – employment,
population and amenity*

Healthy population size

For a Next Level HMO® strategy, we want to ensure a sufficiently large volume of potential tenants. My rule of thumb is upwards of more than 100,000 people in the target town, to ensure a solid, plentiful demographic of the right age group. This doesn't mean less than 100,000 is bad, but it is a good cut-off point with which to begin.

Strong employment options

These 100,000 people in your town, what are they doing? Are they working at all, and in town or commuting elsewhere? Are they studying? To fully understand your source of tenants, answering these questions is vital.

Unless you choose to include a social housing strategy, most of your tenants will be employed; the next question is where. To ensure a healthy volume of tenants, we need at least three *major* local employers from three distinctly different industry sectors.

TOP TIP

Three major employers in an area means that if an industry changes or employment categories fall, you won't be left holding an HMO property with declining demand.

This number is a must – and the larger the employer, the better. But they must also be growing businesses, not declining. Research those employers for future relocation, downsizing or expansion plans, etc.

Confirm how many people they employ, and the demographics. Are they companies that attract lots of young graduates every year, which would annually replenish tenant supply? Don't count companies which primarily employ older professionals living in single households.

LINKING HOMES TO EMPLOYERS

It's possible to directly link your service to one or more of these employers. We have a small HMO in Burnley, where a large distribution hub for a global clothing brand is located: we work with the agency that places workers in shared accommodation. There is a large demand for quality rooms in the area, since the historic stock is underinvested.

Students are also a source of potential tenants, as long as student housing block construction doesn't compromise their availability. If students are viable tenants, we need to know if the universities are thriving, and if they're short of housing. Also, if students want to live in a block or smaller houses.

If there is enough demand, you could offer a larger block – this would definitely come under Next Level HMO® territory. Just remember that university areas have differing student demand, but as long as your target town boasts major employers as well, you will have back-up tenants.

Great local amenities

There are three elements to this: transport links, local shops and social life.

Invariably, we begin our site search within one mile of a train station. Some useful questions to research are:

- How easily could potential tenants get to work?

- Where do the trains go, and how long do they take to get there?

- What is the schedule and frequency – eg do trains run every 10 minutes or once an hour?

- Is it an affordable commute?

If there are no trains, or the location is more than a mile away from a station:

- Are there any other transportation options?

- Guided busway, tram stop or good bus links?

- Has the council invested in good cycle highways?

If tenants prefer to commute by car:

- Is the property close to road links?

- Is there sufficient parking?

The more off-road parking we can provide in such cases, the better, both for tenants and neighbours.

In the wake of the Covid-19 pandemic, a lot of tenants are working from home more than they did previously, but they still need to get around. It would be foolish to assume that transport links have dropped down the list of importance to tenants.

How about shops? Imagine living in the property for a moment and consider:

- How are tenants going to buy groceries?

- Is there a corner shop nearby or supermarket?

- What other local shops would they be interested in – perhaps a takeaway or pharmacy?

Walking distance is preferable for this.

Anything which can benefit tenants' social life should also be included in your appraisal of an area:

- Where can they socialise outside of the property?

- Are there restaurants, cafes, bars, pubs, event spaces, gig venues, art galleries, etc?

Supply versus demand

A good way to gauge the demand for rooms is to access the portals where tenants, landlords and agents advertise. These change from time to time, and different areas often favour one over another.

Let's take a look at some of the more prominent portals.

Spareroom

Spareroom.co.uk is currently the UK's leading portal for room-only accommodation for landlords, agents and tenants. If you have a room to let, or you're a tenant looking for a room or housemate, you can advertise it there.

This gives us the price that tenants consider reasonable, as well as how many existing rooms fit those parameters. You can also assess how many rooms are available and how many people are searching, which enables you to calculate the ratio of prospective tenants to available rooms.

For example, if 200 people are searching for rooms in a town where only 100 rooms are available, that's a ratio of 2:1 – two prospective tenants for every available room. Excellent, but this is only one piece of evidence, so we must keep looking.

Here's how to use it for research:

- Filter the tenant demographic by age, to see who you could attract.

- Filter available properties by postcode, not town name, for available properties. Tenants don't typically restrict their searches to specific towns; they use postcodes. Were you to filter using a town name, the results could appear dramatically different.

- Exclude potentially fake ads from investors testing the marketplace.

- Agents sometimes post more ads and repeat ads so that they get the call over other agents, so exclude these.

Once you have your sights on a property, you could list an advert with 'coming soon' and see what response you get. This is a great way to gauge demand, as you will see how many potential tenants are attracted to your ad and how quickly you get a response.

Ideal Flatmate

Primarily used in major metropolitan areas, Idealflatmate.co.uk is a similar portal to Spareroom. You can use it to calculate the number of rooms available against the number of flatmates looking.

Gumtree

Gumtree.com is used primarily by landlords to secure tenants directly. Some agents do place ads here, but not all. Still, using this can aid your supply/demand ratio calculations regarding the number of rooms available versus people looking in your target area.

Facebook Marketplace

Similar to Gumtree, Facebook Marketplace is a DIY approach. You need a Facebook profile to get started, and you have to know *where* to advertise. Just listing an ad won't get your rooms let. For now, use it to note how many rooms are available and apply them to your list, avoiding duplicates.

Internet search

Search online for 'rooms to rent in [name of town]', just as your potential tenants do, and identify any additional advert sites that are local to your town or are more popular in your region.

The key piece of information you're looking for is how quickly a room lets in this area. None of the portals will tell you outright, but if you monitor these sites on an ongoing basis to see how quickly rooms come and go, you'll get insight into where they let quickly and are in more demand.

By far the best way to get this information outside of analysing data is to speak to agents on the ground who have hands-on, up-to-date knowledge of the current room-rental universe.

Speak to agents

Once you've done your desktop research, it's time to get moving. Call up lettings and estate agents and ask them questions, to get a sense of the marketplace and interview them as potential agents when you're ready to rent:

- What locations, in their experience, do HMO lettings work best?

- What types of properties work?

- What size of HMO works – do their tenants prefer 4/5/6/7-bed, etc?

- Is there a high density of HMOs already in any of the particular areas?

- Are there any areas to avoid?

- Where do most of their tenants work?

- Do they have any corporate contracts?

Their answers will give you a flavour of the area, even potentially open up new ones that your desktop research might be missing.

Visualise the area

Build a map of the place that you are investigating. A simple Ordnance Survey map will do the trick, or you can do it online using a tool such as Google My Maps. Note all of your research on the map using a colour-coded system of employment locations, amenities and transport links, which will give you a clear picture of where is good to look in your town.

These are the two best ways to research your place: a bird's-eye, visual view from a map, and on the ground by speaking to people. Which you prefer depends on you, but both are essential. If you don't like one way, find someone who does to help you. If you cut corners and only pursue one avenue, you may miss an opportunity or make a potentially costly mistake.

Having a partner is a good thing, as it provides another perspective – a sounding board – to ensure you're on the right lines, be it a business partner or mentor.

9
Insight Into People

Once we've identified the towns and cities that meet the three initial criteria of population, employment and amenity, and have identified a consistent or growing demand for rooms, it's time to examine the demographic of our potential tenants.

Who will live in your Next Level HMO® when it's complete?

Assessing the demographic

Return to your list of primary employers and evaluate each one:

- What kind of industry is it?

- What kind of employment does it offer?

- Do employees work in a distribution hub, or pack food boxes?

- Is it a call centre or financial institution?

- Are workers transient or looking for career progression?

- How much do they earn?

- What is the average age group in this type of employment?

- Do employees tend to be single, partnered or have families?

HMOs is a strategy that centres on people looking to share common spaces: primarily comprising single people, with the occasional dual-income, no kids couple. It's worth noting that couples rarely stay long, as they may see HMOs as a stepping-stone to something else; alternatively, if they break up and neither can afford to pay the rent singlehandedly, they may be forced to vacate. (This happened to us in a property in Newcastle, when a couple broke up and both tenants vanished without notice, with two months left on their agreement. Thankfully, we swiftly found replacement tenants so we didn't need to chase the delinquent tenants for the unpaid rent.)

Market research

Often, the most insightful information can be gleaned from interacting directly with people, primarily with tenants. But what if I don't have any tenants yet?

In Chapter 8 we looked at searching online for 'room to rent in [town name]', so you should have a good idea of where tenants are looking and what for. Now it's time to talk to them directly. Go back to those portals and contact the tenants who are advertising to find a room, either messaging them through the platform or calling them if they've listed a contact number in their advert.

Call up lettings agents and ask them to survey their tenants. And if you have tenants in existing properties, send them a survey to complete.

Facebook polls

One effective ploy is to conduct a poll of a local Facebook group for your area. In the search bar on Facebook, type the name of your target town. From among the results, select 'groups' to list all of the groups that contain the name of your town. There will be groups for buying and selling and local community – some public and some which you will have to request to join.

How do you choose the best ones? Facebook kindly tells us how many members each group has and the average number of posts per day.

Note that if you gravitate towards the largest groups with the most activity, your post won't stay at the top long: it'll be lost in the noise of social media. Conversely, if you join a modest-sized group of 100 people or fewer, they are more likely to see your post, but what percentage of those people are renting or looking to rent rooms?

The best way I've found is to search for large groups with moderate activity, and post there. Any group with more than 1,000 people is worth joining to post your poll or a link to your external survey.

Keep a record of where you post, periodically check the results and, if necessary, bump it back to the top of the page. Any comment will return it to the top, including yours, so every few hours or every day, go back in and type something as a comment. Some posters merely type 'bump' to make it rise; others just a full stop.

Now that we know how to get a survey out, how do we construct it and what do we need to know? Below is a list of questions to get you started.

Tenant survey

- Age group – eg 18–24, 25–39, 40–60, etc; or maybe 18–34, 35–49, 50–65, based on your target ages

- Relationship status – eg singles, dual-income no kids

- Education level – eg university student, graduate or school leaver

- Nationality – domestic/foreign; UK citizen/legal immigrant

- Income range – this helps you establish price points, gauge tenants' budgets and financial security, and helps determine their type and level of employment

- Desired features – eg common areas: lounge, kitchen; private or shared bathrooms; disability-friendly features; off-road parking, and one or more spaces; secure storage, including for bicycles

In March 2020 we performed a survey to get an idea of the state of the marketplace. Here are some of the questions we asked to reveal differences in age groups, tenant profiles, geography, etc.

Current status

1. Are you:	☐ A student
	☐ Employed
	☐ Self-employed/contractor
	☐ Unemployed
2. Do you work:	☐ Full-time
	☐ Part-time
	☐ From home

Relocation plans

3. Do you plan to move in the next:	☐ 3 months
	☐ 6 months
	☐ 9 months
	☐ 12 months
	☐ Longer
4. Do you plan to:	☐ Buy a property
	☐ Rent a house
	☐ Rent a flat
	☐ Share a rental

Preferred environment

5. Do you like to spend time with your housemates?	☐ Yes
	☐ No
6. What is the maximum number of people with whom you are willing to share a kitchen?	☐ 2
	☐ 3
	☐ 4
	☐ 5
	☐ 6
	☐ 7
	☐ 8
7. Are you happy to share a bathroom?	☐ Yes
	☐ No

8. How would you prefer to report maintenance problems?	☐	Online
	☐	Phone
	☐	Text
	☐	Social media
9. Are you happy with the Wi-Fi in your house?	☐	Yes
	☐	No

Work/travel

10. Do you own a:	☐	Car
	☐	Motorcycle
	☐	Bicycle
	☐	Other means of transport
11. What is your main mode of transport to work:	☐	Bus
	☐	Tram
	☐	Train
	☐	Car
	☐	Bike
	☐	Walk
12. How long does it take you to get to work?		
13. If bus, tram or train, how long does it take you to get to the station/stop?		
14. Are you content with your commute?	☐	Yes
	☐	No – too long
15. If you work from home, what features do you require?	☐	Desk in bedroom
	☐	Separate office space, studio, etc
16. What improvements would you like over your current set-up?	☐	Faster Wi-Fi
	☐	More desk space
	☐	Better lighting
	☐	More comfortable surroundings
	☐	Other

17. When you do travel, what's your main mode of transport?	☐ Bus ☐ Tram ☐ Train ☐ Car ☐ Bike ☐ Walk

When choosing a room

18. How many rooms did you view before choosing your current house?	☐ 1–5 ☐ 6–10 ☐ 10
19. From 1–10, rate the importance of these when choosing a room:	☐ Number of housemates ☐ Relationship with existing housemates ☐ En-suite bathroom ☐ Travel time to work/university ☐ Distance from local shops ☐ Parking ☐ Cycle storage ☐ Room location within house ☐ Kitchen size ☐ Lounge area size ☐ Bedroom size ☐ Own cooking facilities ☐ Personal storage space ☐ Personal desk space ☐ Wi-Fi

Additional services

20. What added services does your landlord provide?	☐ Communal space cleaning ☐ Cleaning of your room and private spaces ☐ Bed linen ☐ General laundry ☐ Organised social events ☐ Perks sold to you before you move in

21. What added services would you be willing to pay a premium for?	☐ Communal space cleaning
	☐ Cleaning of your room and private spaces
	☐ Bed linen
	☐ General laundry
	☐ Organised social events
	☐ Perks sold to you before you move in

Qualifying questions

How old are you?	eg:
	☐ 18–24
	☐ 25–39
	☐ 40–60 etc
	or maybe:
	☐ 18–34
	☐ 35–49
	☐ 50–65
What is your postcode?	
What is your county?	

For a summary of the results and to be included in future versions of the Shared Living Survey, head over to www.sharedlivingsurvey.co.uk/nextlevellandlord to register to receive a link to send to your future tenants.

TENANT PROFILE
The HMO Platform

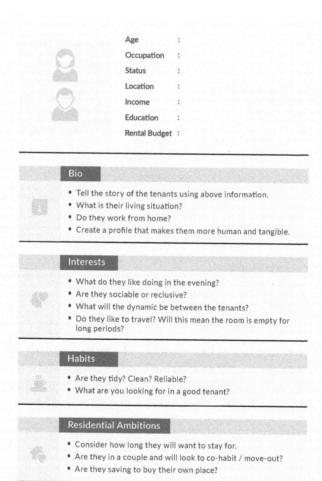

Age :

Occupation :

Status :

Location :

Income :

Education :

Rental Budget :

Bio

- Tell the story of the tenants using above information.
- What is their living situation?
- Do they work from home?
- Create a profile that makes them more human and tangible.

Interests

- What do they like doing in the evening?
- Are they sociable or reclusive?
- What will the dynamic be between the tenants?
- Do they like to travel? Will this mean the room is empty for long periods?

Habits

- Are they tidy? Clean? Reliable?
- What are you looking for in a good tenant?

Residential Ambitions

- Consider how long they will want to stay for.
- Are they in a couple and will look to co-habit / move-out?
- Are they saving to buy their own place?

Figure 9.1: High-value tenant profile

In the meantime, try doing this research for yourself. Once a year we can go out to the entire country to ask the same set of questions and get a UK-wide picture of what's working, what isn't and how we can improve as landlords.

Once you know this information, you can begin putting together a picture of who your tenant is – create your tenant avatar – listing their features that you can pin to the wall of your office or desk to remind yourself who you are targeting as a customer (Figure 9.1).

Once you have this nailed, you can design your HMO to fit the types of people who are likely to live in your Next Level HMO®: your high-value tenants.

10
Insight Into Planning

The planning system is a big beast and can sometimes feel like a game rigged against us as property developers. When you've worked for two years on a project, the moment you get that final permission through – the green light, and hopefully the route to profit – it can be a source of joy.

The aim of this chapter is to demystify planning permissions, and how we can use them strategically to create Next Level HMOs.

Fundamentally, there are two routes to go down when doing a project: the easy way and the hard way! Most HMO investors will opt for the easy way, using government-granted permitted development rights, because it almost always ensures that you have permission to do your project. But this doesn't garner the same rewards as taking the road less travelled: a full planning application.

The easy way: permitted development rights

Planning applications are determined by council planning departments which are, on the whole, over-worked, understaffed and underpaid, making it virtually impossible for them to determine whether every single change is acceptable. In 1995, the Government introduced the General Permitted Development Order, which streamlines certain planning permissions.[12] Such rights permit things such as satellite dish installation, changing or adding windows, erecting a fence, and so on. Bigger projects, such as extensions and loft conversions, and changes of use also may be permitted development.

These permitted development rights are the starting point in maximising a building via a step-by-step approach, as we generally want to use them first before applying for full planning permission. Why? Because it prevents them from being removed if we do seek full planning approval.

There are two types of permitted development:

---

12   www.legislation.gov.uk/uksi/1995/418/contents/made

- Deemed consent

- Prior approval via prior notification (a short planning application)

Deemed consent is a property developer's dream right, because you can go ahead and do the works without seeking permission. Examples of this are loft conversions and extensions under a certain size, and (believe it or not) creating flats above shops.

The prior approval process is a little more involved, as you are required to submit a prior notification. This dramatically limits the tests that you need to pass to get permission.

Maximising houses through permitted development

The number one rule when creating Next Level HMOs and co-living is to *maximise the building*. We're not talking making everything the bare minimum size or piling people into small rooms on mattresses on the floor (that sort of thing still happens, but thankfully is being stamped out).

As mentioned previously, the first and most effective way is to use the permitted development rights on our property before thinking about full planning application. Here are some ways to use those rights for C3 houses and C4 and *sui generis* HMOs.

Rear extensions

This is an easy way to add space and bedrooms to a property. Single-storey extensions are easy, thanks to being simple structures atop simple foundations. They can be massive too, especially if a detached house.

You can extend out from the rear of the original house, meaning the building as it stood on 1 July 1948. If it has already been extended, some of your permitted development rights will have been used already. When you calculate the area that you intend to create, this can't be more than 50% of the curtilage (grounds) of the property, but it can be the full width of the house – as long as the extension is only connected to walls facing the rear of the property, and not to the side.

TOP TIP

If you have an attached outhouse or outrigger, be careful not to extend to the side of these, as they require full planning permission.

Table 10.1 shows how far back you can go, and whether you need to submit a prior notification or not.

Table 10.1: *Single-storey rear extension*[13]

Semi-detached and terraced houses	Detached houses	Type of right
3 m	4 m	Permitted development – do it
6 m	8 m	Prior notification – ask, then do it

If you need to submit a prior notification, the council will consult your direct neighbours either side of you: as long as they don't object, the decision is out of the council's hands; it can go ahead. If the neighbours do comment or object, then it is back in the hands of the planning officer to decide (this period is 42 days).

Table 10.2: *Double-storey rear extension*[14]

All house types	Type of right
3 m	Permitted development – do it

Table 10.2 shows that this type of extension can be 3 m in length and the full width of the house – but there must be a long rear garden with at least 7 m of open space remaining, once the works are completed.

---

13 See the Town and Country Planning (General Permitted Development) (England) Order 2015 (as amended) Schedule 2, Part 1, Class A: www.legislation.gov.uk/uksi/2015/596/schedule/2/made.

14 See the Town and Country Planning (General Permitted Development) (England) Order 2015 (as amended) Schedule 2, Part 1, Class A: www.legislation.gov.uk/uksi/2015/596/schedule/2/made.

Side extensions

Extending sideways works well if you have an end-terraced property or a side garden. The extension can be up to 50% of the width of the original house, and only single-storey. Anything else requires full planning permission beforehand.

Loft extensions and conversions

Loft conversions are a good way to maximise the height of your building, assuming there is enough head height to do so. It can be done internally, without permission, as can the addition of rooflights on both the front and back of the house. If you want to increase the loft's volume, you can extend to the rear and sides of the house, but you cannot project beyond the front elevation.

The roof extension would likely be a flat-roof dormer, or potentially a pitched roof if smaller. Dormers can add up to 40 m^3 to terraced houses and 50 m^3 to semi-detached and detached properties. That's a lot of space to add to an existing building! (Our aim is normally to add two bedrooms via loft extension.)

The hard way: maximising property through planning gain

Once the property has been maximised under permitted development, it's possible to achieve further uplift in value through planning permission. This means either getting planning approved for a C4 HMO in an Article 4 area, or *sui generis* planning approved for a larger HMO property.

NB: An Article 4 direction doesn't stop you entirely. Planning permission is still possible, as long as you comply with the council's planning policies.

Figure 10.1 shows the planning stages of going from a house to creating a small and then a large HMO.

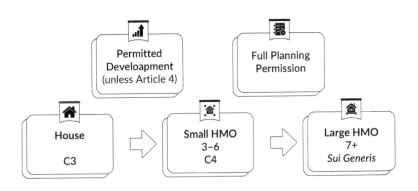

Figure 10.1: Converting houses to HMOs

As mentioned previously, planning permission is required for most external and some internal changes to buildings in the UK; it's also required for change of use. It's a rules-based system, so we need to know the rules to know how to play.

You can only pass the test if you learn and follow the rules of the council's planning policy. Councils that have what we call 'binary policies' are the most straightforward. These contain rules that are black and white – either they work, or they don't.

A key rule to determine is the council's policy on achieving a 'mixed and balanced community': how many HMOs are allowed in a given area. If this is determined by formula, you can calculate whether the council believes there are enough HMOs already – a saturation calculation. If no formula is provided, decisions are discretionary, and the council has wiggle room to refuse your application.

For example, a binary policy might state: 'There can be no more than 10% of HMOs within a 50-metre radius surrounding the property.' Figure 10.2 shows how one council could calculate it.

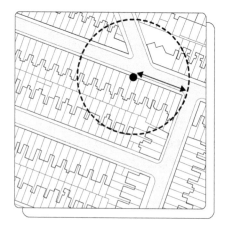

Figure 10.2: Identifying the area surrounding the application property

Each council has its own method that may differ slightly. Some may insist on a radius of 100 m or 200 m or have a 20% threshold, while others may calculate their percentage using a straight line up and down the street. The place to find this policy is in your local council's core strategy or supplementary planning document concerning HMOs on the council's website. Be aware: there may not be a policy to find!

TOP TIP

Your local council may have a fixed formula to calculate how many HMOs it permits within a specific-sized area. For example:

HMO density: No. of HMOs ÷ No. of houses = % of HMOs

Parking

Quite often we see a policy that applies a minimum requirement of 0.5 spaces per room, meaning the council allows that not all tenants drive. In such an instance, an eight-bed HMO requires only four spaces. But if the property lacks four off-road spaces, where else can they park? If the property is a house, there is an assumption that it already supports several cars – possibly three – so in the eight-bed example, you are only adding one additional car. The test becomes: can the local area cope with one extra car?

If the property is in an area where the council is encouraging public transport use, this can be argued in your favour with fewer spaces. But the council may not have a policy at all, which means it's hard for them to enforce a large number of spaces.

Bin storage

Similar to parking requirements, the number of bins or bin storage volume may or may not be established policy. If you're doing a *sui generis* large HMO application, you may be required to provide larger commercial Eurobins, or buy more wheelie bins and work out where they will go.

If you do a *sui generis* application and the bins can't be stored to the rear of the property, that complicates matters. We ideally look for properties with side or rear access, where bins can be wheeled out and collected.

Cycle storage

As with the previous two points, there may not be a policy for this in place. It's safe to assume that for large HMO applications, the council will ask for covered, secure cycle storage for one bike per bedroom.

Amenity space

This generally follows licensing standards. If you can get a licence on the property, you'll usually pass this test, but check with your local council to be certain. It used to be that planning and licensing departments didn't talk to each other; but licensing departments are increasingly consulted in the planning application process.

Go for the 'no'

Once you submit your application, it takes about five weeks to learn which way the council is leaning. If it's towards no, they may ask you to withdraw your application on the basis that they intend to refuse you. When this happens, we always push back, because as long as we have been correctly advised by our planning consultant, we know we are in the right.

If they know you intend to continue with your application, you may find room for compromise. When a council refuses your application, they will supply you with the reasons; everything else, except these reasons, is then acceptable by default. Once we know these, we can do one of two things:

- Resubmit the application at no extra charge, with proposed solutions (within a year for the 'free go').

- Appeal the reasons for refusal, if we believe that the council has got it wrong, to have a planning inspector decide.

Accordingly, if they say you are going to be refused, go for the no, then go back and fix or fight it.

TOP TIP

Full planning permission on HMOs takes eight weeks from the date that the council validates your application. Larger or complex schemes can take thirteen weeks.

Permitted development for commercial buildings

The main difference between permitted development for houses and commercial buildings is that you can make changes to the fabric of a house. For commercial buildings, we can use permitted development rights to change the use of the property, but they don't allow for external changes.

We want to maximise the property for residential use, and there are quite a few rights that we can use to turn commercial property into residential. Under the current government, permitted development rights have changed quite a lot recently, including the ability to add storeys to commercial and residential properties. The new rights specifically rule out changing these new additions to HMOs using permitted development. It is important to stay on top of these rights, as more opportunities or restrictions could appear at any time.

In addition to the residential C Class, the only classes which have permitted development rights are Class E and *sui generis*.

Class E and *sui generis*

Class E is the amalgamation of use classes that used to be known as classes A1, A2, A3 and B1: Shops, financial and professional services, restaurants and cafes, offices, research and development of products or processes, industrial processes compatible with a residential area, clinics, health centres, crèches, day nurseries, day centres, gymnasiums or area for indoor sports and recreations (excluding swimming pools and skating rinks).

The only type of property that falls under *sui generis* that we can convert under permitted development is amusement arcades and casinos.

At the time of writing, the current permitted development rights are useable:

- Class G – retail, betting office or payday loan shop to mixed-use
- Class M – shop (former A1/A2/A3) to dwelling houses
- Class N – specified *sui generis* uses to dwelling houses (arcades and casinos)
- Class O – offices (former B1(a)) to dwelling houses

Class G

What's colloquially known as the 'two flats above a shop' or 'shops with uppers' permission allows us to look at the retail classes and make it mixed-use, to form two dwellings above an existing shop. These flats could then become small HMOs, up to six people each, assuming no Article 4 direction is in place to restrict that change.

The Class G right is amazing in two other ways. It is deemed consent, which means you don't need to request approval or permission; you can just go ahead and do it. It also works on listed buildings, so it opens up some otherwise challenging opportunities.

Class M and Class N

Known informally as 'retail or casino to resi', Classes M and N cover conversion of former shops or amusement arcades into houses or flats. This requires a prior notification to be submitted, and only works outside of the primary high street and for properties up to 150 m².

You will need to prove that the property is not subject to flooding, poor highway safety or ground contamination, and potentially provide the relevant surveys. It also doesn't work on listed buildings.

TOP TIP

To fully convert a shop, you can apply for Class G permitted development rights first, do the upstairs conversion, then apply for Class M to convert the downstairs.

Class O

This is probably the most well-known and used permitted development right, colloquially known as 'office to resi'. The biggest difference between this and the other classes is that there is no size limitation, so whether it's 150 m² or 15,000 m², it doesn't matter.

It is subject to the same tests as Class M, but replaces the condition about the primary high street with a noise condition. You may have to perform a noise assessment to test whether there will be any impact on your intended residents from surrounding commercial sources.

If you are in a residential area this tends not to be a problem, but if you are next to a factory or metal workshop, this may be a factor.

Prior notification pointers

Don't try to do this yourself unless it's a simple project; use a planning consultant to deal with this for you. Once the application has been submitted with the correct payment, the clock starts ticking the next day: day one of your 56-day period.

An advantage in the prior approvals process is that the onus is on the council to come back to you within these 56 days; if they don't, permission is assumed to have been granted, unlike a normal planning application which must be determined one way or another.[15]

The final caveat is that you must *complete* the conversion within three years of approval date, whereas normally in planning you have three years to *commence* the building works.

All of these permitted development rights are accurate at the time of writing, but it's always smart to ensure you're up-to-date. Plus, there are some additional nuances not mentioned here. That's why we recommend you use a planning consultant for this type of conversion.

Figure 10.3 shows the planning stages of taking a commercial building to HMO.

---

15 See the Town and Country Planning (General Permitted Development) (England) Order 2015, Schedule 2, Part 3, Class V, Paragraph W (11)(c): www.legislation.gov.uk/uksi/2015/596/schedule/2/paragraph/W/made

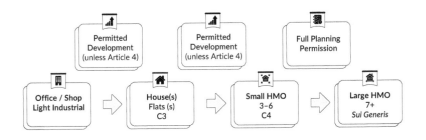

Figure 10.3: Converting commercial properties to HMOs

Full planning permission to maximise a property

As mentioned previously, once we possess the permitted development permission on a commercial building, we have the right to change the *inside* of the property, but not the outside – so we might want to submit a full planning application to make external alterations, such as install new doors, windows and / or rooflights to improve natural lighting in conjunction with the proposed internal layout. We may also want to add extensions that don't fall under permitted development and require planning permission or that alter the front of a property where there are no such rights.

If you're going for a large HMO, the last piece of the puzzle is usually a full planning application: *sui generis*. You must ensure that you meet the *sui generis* HMO application criteria discussed previously. The exception is creating a fallback position by legally occupying the building with the same number of tenants in a number of apartments as you want in the HMO – then the council should approve a *sui generis* application, given that there has been no material change of use.

CONVERTING A HAIR SALON TO MIXED-USE COMMERCIAL/HMO

The property was a hairdressing salon with a two-bed flat above it: a mixed-use building that the vendor was keen to sell quickly. On the market with a residential estate agent in 2018, it was being advertised online, but wasn't among the commercial listings – so investors looking for commercial property weren't seeing it, and homeowners wouldn't know what to do with it. That meant no interested parties.

The tenant upstairs, a council tenant, had been there for as long as the vendor could remember, and the vendor was not only not charging the full rent the tenant was entitled to from the council, but was even paying the tenant's utilities. Somewhere along the line this property had stopped performing.

It was on the market for £95,000 and we agreed on £91,000, on a street where other residential properties of comparable size were selling for £120,000-plus.

The shop downstairs was use Class A1 and underused: the front portion enjoyed steady use, but the rear of the shop was a rabbit warren and used inefficiently. It was not in a primary retail location, so Class M permitted development rights were available to us. Indeed, as the end terrace of a residential street and a corner shop-style, the whole building would be suited to full residential conversion; but by keeping an element of commercial use, we could get the entire building valued commercially instead of just as a £120,000 house.

The building was the same length as the other terraced houses, but had a sizeable, dilapidated, detached rear garage which, being on the ground floor, meant the garage was also classed as retail use.

The fallback position

Permitted development doesn't always provide exactly want we want in a project: if we go straight in with the desired scheme, it's less likely to be approved. But permitted development can give us a fallback position which can be used to help get us what we want through full planning.

USING FALLBACK IN THE SALON DEVELOPMENT

The strategy was to submit the prior notification for Class M to convert the ground floor into three flats. This went through with no hiccups at all, permitting conversion of the hairdressers to two flats, and the garage into a third.

But under permitted development we were not allowed to alter the garage's exterior. Knowing the council would prefer we upgrade the look, our fallback position was to suggest upgrading it to an attractive brick-built building to match the surroundings.

We resubmitted the planning application to include this, asking that we also be permitted to attach it to the main building, knowing it didn't change the appearance from the street.

While undoubtedly appealing to the council, our first application was refused, based on the design. We had designed a pitched roof for the rear extension, and they wanted a flat roof, but they didn't object to attaching the buildings. Believing the refusal to be incorrect, we appealed it and resubmitted with the flat roof possibility. Both were approved, giving us two designs to choose from!

We designed part of the ground-floor shop as an en-suite bedroom and converted the upstairs flat into three en-suite bedrooms. We demolished and rebuilt the garage, attached it to the main house, and installed a large, communal kitchen diner. The shop was refurbished and left as a blank canvas for a new commercial tenant.

Voilà! We now had a shop and a four-bed HMO with full planning permission.

We spent roughly £90,000 on top of the £91,000 purchase price, on a property that was subsequently valued at £230,000. This yielded nearly £50,000 profit, which remains there as equity. The project was refinanced at 75% loan-to-value (LTV) with a commercial bank, based on the commercial valuation of the property as a mixed-use scheme turning over £2,500 per month.

It's rare to achieve a commercial valuation on a four-bed HMO, but this happened because it was part of a mixed-use scheme.

Co-living as a planning concept

Some councils cover seemingly every possible HMO feature under the sun in their policy, while others don't even mention HMO or shared living in theirs. How does the current planning system work for the growing co-living marketplace? We spoke with colleagues, other professionals and larger developers about what is happening.

We asked: should there be a new planning class for co-living, or should we pigeonhole it into the existing framework? The consensus was that there is no need for a new planning class: we just need to follow the lead of those councils that take co-living seriously and introduce high standards of living for the future tenants of such properties.

The most relevant example of co-living is among students. In older and more established universities, shared housing is common and has become a big problem for councils, so they legislated to bring in Article 4 areas and licensing with the aim to elevate standards. What this in fact accomplished was to make it hard for new landlords to enter the market. The supply of new, shared properties dried up, while demand kept increasing. When demand massively outstrips supply, there is no incentive for existing landlords to improve their properties.

When larger developers started submitting applications for sizeable student blocks to meet demand, they needed regulating, so the councils brought in a planning policy for large student blocks which were essentially *sui generis*, large HMOs. Councils prefer this kind of development because it encourages students to live in one place rather than being spread out over the city in smaller houses. When students move back into the blocks, it releases more housing for families.

The same is happening with large HMOs in the main towns. London is taking the lead on this, with the largest population. As of mid-2019, London has 5,700 people per square kilometre, the median age being just over 36 years.[16] Most of those rent, with the largest rental group nationally being 35%, falling into the 25–34 age range in 2017.[17] It is only natural that as housing becomes less affordable, co-living becomes more affordable and desirable. This large, growing population needs somewhere to live, and although councils try to restrict new HMOs by way of Article 4 policies, they still need this type of accommodation. They need policies to guide developers to create what the council wants. When this happens, we can create

16   'Population estimates for the UK, England and Wales, Scotland and Northern Ireland: mid-2019' (Office for National Statistics, 2020), www.ons.gov.uk/peoplepopulationandcommunity/populationandmigration/populationestimates/bulletins/annualmidyearpopulationestimates/mid2019estimates, accessed 11 November 2020

17   'UK private rented sector: 2018' (Office for National Statistics, 2019), www.ons.gov.uk/economy/inflationandpriceindices/articles/ukprivaterentedsector/2018#tenants, accessed 11 November 2020

large co-living developments, help to free up housing for families, and create a more balanced community.

THE COLLECTIVE'S APPROACH

Leading the way in large HMOs is The Collective: a large developer which only does projects of 200-plus bedrooms. The Scott Baker Properties team met with its planning and strategic communications director and former town planner, James Penfold, to discuss their projects and how they handle planning permissions.

Once The Collective identifies a site, its first key point is to engage with both the local planning department and the community before going in for planning. This is a different approach to when there are permitted development rights to fall back on; without those, it is pivotal to get both council and community on board. If the council sees that you take community engagement seriously, it tends to view your scheme more favourably. It also helps to obtain letters of support from the community when you file your application.

The Collective takes its ideas and plans to the local community and hosts events, knowing from experience that initially, they can view new development with hostility, mainly because they don't understand it. The Collective solicits its opinions and integrates as many of them into the scheme as possible. When it returns, the community recognises that they have been heard, and the scheme has improved as a result.

This approach obviously helps The Collective gain planning permission, but it also sits at the heart of what it wants to do. As well as having its own internal community, The Collective believes that a large co-living scheme needs to be part of the wider community. It asks: how can the development benefit and give back to the local area?

The Collective learned a lot through trial and error, and has demonstrated to the London councils it works with that it has the desire to learn and improve – so much so that it worked with the Greater London Authority to develop a new co-living policy for London-based developments. The full policy, Policy H18, from the *Draft London Plan*,[18] makes for interesting reading: it covers a lot of points including amenities, management and a sense of community, as well as making a cash contribution towards affordable housing.

I would argue that all councils need to proactively implement HMO policies to provide a clear indication of what they will accept, and set standards. While larger cities are seeing large co-living developments going through, those councils have implemented policies reactively, invariably led by developers trying to do something new and the council struggling to find a way to manage it.

As developers, when we operate in a grey area this creates opportunity, but it also creates uncertainty, which leads to risk. For now, we know the rules currently in place and the permitted development we

---

18 London Plan Team, *The Draft London Plan: Consolidated changes version July 2019* (Mayor of London, 2019), www.london.gov.uk/sites/default/files/draft_london_plan_-_consolidated_changes_version_july_2019.pdf, accessed 11 November 2020

can take advantage of while it is in place. But being a good developer here isn't enough. We need to be good operators and managers of HMOs: the better our reputation with a council, the better our chances are of getting planning permission through as our businesses, ideas and schemes grow.

We welcome and encourage these changes.

11
Insight Into Property

A re you one of these people who happily spends hours trawling through Rightmove, looking at houses? If so, you'll love this aspect of the Tenant First method. Some people consider looking for properties a real headache, while others absolutely adore it.

I'm definitely someone who loves to look at deals, but not a fan of looking for a needle in a haystack. I much prefer deals to be presented to me on a platter and to come up with a planning strategy, then analyse and appraise them. My business partner Niall would happily scroll through online portals, but when it comes to appraising, he would rather throw his laptop into a fire to avoid looking at a spreadsheet.

I like sourcing to be systemised, which we're going to address in this chapter: the eight steps to find a Next Level HMO®. I all but guarantee that if you do what I suggest, you will find deals:

1. Create your specific hunting brief

2. Work the agents

3. Network

4. Use websites effectively

5. Bid at auctions

6. Use vendor finance and lease options

7. Leverage online tools

8. Leverage sourcing agents

Let's look at each one of these in detail.

Create your specific hunting brief

It's difficult to start your search if you haven't defined what you're looking for. Being specific is the most important part of sourcing properties for HMO use. Start with the end in mind: how big do you need this property to be to meet your needs? That's your first calculation (Figure 11.1).

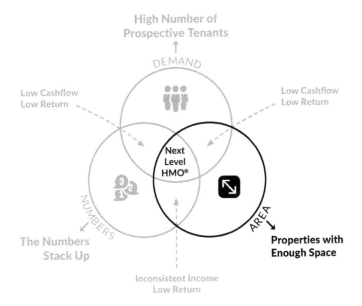

Figure 11.1: The DNA of a Next Level HMO® - area

Let's look at a target room size of minimum 10.5 m^2 for a single-occupancy living bedroom: ie, the tenant is deemed to be able to sleep and live in the room, reducing the need for a separate living room (Table 11.1).

To hit our target size and specification of property, we can see it needs it to be about 157 m^2 when completed. Note, that because we can still do works to extend an existing property, it doesn't always need to be 157 m^2 to start with.

Table 11.1: Goal: eight-bed HMO property[19]

Target room size	10.5 m² to be single-occupancy living bedrooms
Target communal space	large combined communal kitchen/dining/living area
Bedroom	**10.5 m²** x 8 rooms = 84 m²
En-suite bathroom	**3 m²** x 8 = 24 m²
Communal kitchen (larger than the regulations require)	15 m² x 1 = 15 m²
Communal living area (larger than the regulations require)	20 m² x 1 = 20 m²
Total size required for rooms	143 m²
Corridor space	~10% of total room size (143 m²) = 14.3 m²
Total size on completion	157.3 m²

Let's work backwards now, given what we know is possible permitted development-wise. If this is a house-to-HMO conversion, we can do loft and rear extensions:

- Loft conversion – ideally two loft bedrooms, 10.5 m² bed + 3 m² bath = 13.5 m² x 2 = 27 m²

- Rear extension – this can be 6 m long and the width of the house. Most houses are at least 5 m wide, so that's an estimated 30 m² extension

If we subtract the 27 m² loft size, plus the 30 m² estimated extension size, from 157 m², 100 m² is our starting point

19 These areas may be determined by you or taken from the HMO licensing standards.

for the existing building size. When talking to agents, there is no point looking at properties less than 100 m² to create the eight-bed HMO we've targeted. (We generally don't look to convert a house unless there is space to eventually accommodate seven bedrooms.)

Now it's time to construct your hunting brief. Get the details down on paper before talking to agents. Aside from the size, include:

- The postcode locations where you are looking

- Photos of the types of property you want

- A photo of you

- Your contact details.

The hunting brief is simple and effective, *but don't simply email it* – it'll get lost among the fifty other emails the agent has received that day. Print it off, get in the car and go hand it to the agent. When they know precisely what your parameters are, you'll be the first person they call when the right property crosses their desk.

(We gave our hunting brief to our agents in Warrington when we first started looking. One agent kept our printed copy atop her in-tray so that it was always in front of her. That is where you want yours to be!)

Work the agents

Property is a people, not a bricks-and-mortar, business. Remember this when you start looking for properties. This is especially important to keep in mind when working with agents, as that relationship can get you deals well in advance of anyone else.

Working with agents is a more hands-off approach to sourcing, as you aren't physically searching for properties. Instead, if you nurture your relationship with agent, they will bring properties to you.

TOP TIP

The Beer Test: How many agents do you know well enough to go for a beer with them? This is where you want your relationship to be.

How do we become agents' number one investor? Why bring a deal to us, with all the other investors out there? Not every investor is continuously looking: some will have deals under way, while others may have run out of money, and others still won't be proactive enough to see properties.

It's your job to be the ideal investor for the agent: don't waste their time, and complete on deals. Put yourself in their shoes: an investor who takes properties off their hands quickly and easily, with no chain, is someone with whom they're eager to work.

When you first contact an estate agent, you want to identify who among them is the go-getter: who will actively bring you deals. Not all agents have one, but it's fairly easy to spot them. Walk into the agency and scan the properties on the wall. The person who approaches to assist you first is likely a go-getter.

Your goal is to become best buddies with the manager or valuer/appraiser: the person who goes out to a property *before* it goes to market.

BEFRIEND YOUR APPRAISER

When I was actively sourcing properties in Warrington a few years ago, I developed a great relationship with one appraiser and he brought me quite a few deals. He would call me and we'd go for dinner and beers, as we lived near each other. He would also call when he was going to measure up a property and take marketing photos, asking if I'd like to go along.

Of course! I would see a property before it went to market and could put an offer in that worked for me, getting first refusal. In a hot market, this is invaluable.

Be systematic in your approach to building these relationships, so you don't leave anything on the table. List all the agents in the area, and plan your attack. Divide them into small groups and focus on these one at a time. Use all methods of communication: phone, email and visit in-person, to make your presence known but not unwelcome. Take treats to the office and become memorable. Impress them by keeping tabs on their likes, dislikes, family, holidays, etc and you'll quickly become their favourite.

Lettings agents are also a good place to follow up, because they are the first to know if one of their landlords is looking to sell: they can bring your potential deals direct to the vendor.

The commercial agent is a different fish. They are generally slower because the market is not as fluid: they don't have the volume of transactions that residential agents field. Still, they do have new opportunities coming to market reasonably consistently. It's important to be clear on the commercial opportunities you're looking for and create a specific hunting brief for these too, specifying that your prime objective is opportunities with permitted development rights.

In summary, it's all about relationship. There is a great book that explains this well, *How to Win Friends and Influence People*, by Dale Carnegie.[20] I thoroughly recommend this book for all aspects of building relationships.

---

20   D Carnegie, *How to Win Friends and Influence People* (Vermilion, 2006)

Network

Ever bought a property directly from a vendor you met at a networking event? We have.

While there was a delay between the event and the purchase – about two years – it was a great little deal. We were approached because they knew we invested in modest deals in Burnley, and their son was selling there. We weren't really looking but became interested on learning about the deal.

They wanted £36,000 for what we knew was worth £55,000, because we own a similar property a five-minute walk away. The council at the time was also offering interest-free loans up to £20,000, which meant we could buy the property using investor cash and borrow the money to do it up from the council for ten years, interest-free: a no-money-down deal. We turned it into a three-bed, small HMO ('mini-mo'), which was rented to workers at the clothing brand distribution hub.

If you want these sorts of deals, get out and network!

Try networking on a regular basis in the area in which you want to invest. If there is a regular monthly meet-up, go at least every other month so that people start to recognise you and learn what you do.

Make a point of going to networking events where you live, if you don't live where you invest. This is an easier way to meet like-minded people more regularly; you can build those relationships between meetings as well. Long-lasting friendships and business relationships are not made in the room, but in the meetings in-between.

Use websites effectively

Rightmove.co.uk, Zoopla.co.uk and Onthemarket. com all do similar things, each with their own strengths and weaknesses. This is a reactive way of finding property, because you're viewing an advert of a property that has already gone to market and competing against others who also see its potential.

There are two ways we recommend you use property websites to see deals:

- Be alerted to new listings and act quickly

- Look for old listings that have languished and offer the vendor fresh, creative possibilities.

Act quickly

Ideally, your agent will have brought a property to you before listing it; but if not, the goal is to be one of the first to view and offer.

To do this, set up your search areas on these three high-profile websites, and have them automatically email you as soon as a new listing hits the site that fits your criteria.

Look for old listings

The other way to use portals is to work backwards. Instead of viewing the newest listings, reverse the search to see the oldest first. Refine your search as necessary, view what's sticking on the market, and call the agent to find out why. Maybe you can find a creative solution and negotiate a good deal.

While Rightmove, Zoopla and Onthemarket are the top three sites, the listing preferences of agents do change, and there are more. Some properties will appear on multiple portals while others only show up on one, so don't settle on one and assume they're all the same. Facebook and Gumtree are worth a look, for example, while Propertylink.estatesgazette.com features commercial property and land.

Take some time to explore what other sites might feature properties in your target investment town(s).

Bid at auctions

Auctions are not for the faint-hearted. There are strict buying criteria that make it an attractive venue in which to sell. As a purchaser, if your bid is accepted, you have legally exchanged on the property and are obliged to complete on it, generally within 28 days. You need to be prepared to put down 10% cash on the day, as well as provide your solicitor's details.

The main reasons people choose to sell at auction are a quick, guaranteed sale, and because bidding can inflate the starting price. The risks include a property not selling or selling for less than the vendor hopes; but vendors typically set a reserve price to prevent the property from being sold at too low a figure. Auction attendees are furnished a guide price on the day to entice them, but which legally cannot be more than 10% lower than a reserve price. For example, if the guide price is £100,000, then the reserve price is probably £110,000. In some circumstances, the vendor may not opt to set a reserve, which can get bidders excited, thinking there is a deal opportunity.

You can offer before the auction, but there's normally no negotiation. You'll probably get just a yes or no, and could end up bidding against yourself if you keep offering more beforehand. You can also bid after the auction on any lots which don't sell. (That's what I often do, figuring the vendor is now more motivated to sell.)

One property we bought through auction, we managed to buy before *and* after the auction.

BUYING AT AUCTION

The auction was on 20 July 2016, long before our vision of Next Level HMOs, and there was an exciting bustle about the place. Lot numbers 23 and 31 were our targets: two-bed terrace houses in Burnley. The idea was to offer no more than £20,000 each. Bidding started on each one with vigour, and both went for well over our highest offers, securing £25,500 and £23,000 respectively.

Disheartened, I flicked through the auction catalogue and noticed lot 41, a dilapidated property in Warrington, just down the road from Central Station. While it looked interesting as a potential HMO, I wasn't about to bid there and then – I only had £3,000 available on my credit card to use as a deposit, and the guide price was £78,000. I'd need at least £8,000 on hand.

When the lot came up, bids were offered from £78,000 to £82,000. When the auctioneer announced a bid of £84,000, the bidding paused and I assumed it had sold – but it hadn't. Instead, the auctioneer withdrew the property: clearly, it had not hit the reserve price. I made my next assumption, that the bidder of £84,000 would find the auctioneer and try to do a deal. With nothing left to interest us, we got up and headed to the lifts. When the lift doors opened, an elderly couple followed us inside. I smiled and said 'Hi, did you win anything?' The woman replied:

'No. We were actually here to sell, and the property we were selling didn't go.'

'I'm sorry to hear that. What was it?'

135

'A three-bed semi-detached property in Warrington.'

It's rare to meet a vendor at an auction where there's a possibility to do a deal directly. I pressed for more details and learned that she had been left the property by her aunt, and it was in good repair, including a new roof. They chose to manage the property themselves and when the existing tenant moved out, they let it to a family. The tenants moved in, they stopped by a few weeks later to make sure everything was OK, then left them to it.

Several months later, the police phoned to inform them the house had been turned into a cannabis farm. Black mould, no toilet, holes in the walls and ceilings, and rotting floorboards where rain had leaked in and pooled.

'Sorry to hear about all of that,' I said. 'So you're looking to pass this on, aren't you? I saw the guide price was £78,000, so does that mean you're looking for around £87,000?'

'Yes!' she said, perking up. 'That would do it.'

'I do invest in the area, so I'll have a look. Maybe I'll buy it from you.'

Several days passed, until I went online to see if the property was up for a post-auction bid. There it was, lot 37. With no auction scheduled for August, it was listed among the properties being featured for September.

I rang up the auctioneer and asked for a special visit, as there wouldn't be any block viewings until closer to the auction date. The auctioneer wasn't particularly interested, preferring to wait. I explained that I had crossed paths with the vendor, so he scheduled a viewing. I invited our builder to accompany us and do an estimate, and calculated we could do this project if we bought it for £87,000: a great price for a property in that street, and just what the vendor wanted.

We put forward an offer, and it was accepted. We exchanged a week later.

That property became our second ever HMO: six bedrooms, all en-suite, with rooms from 6.5 m to 12 m². Not exactly how I would do it again, but a great property with happy tenants. We spent roughly £80,000 on it and the subsequent initial revaluation, a hybrid valuation (which we'll cover in Chapter 12), was at £180,000.

Knowing what we know now, four years later, we went for and achieved *sui generis* planning permission. The property was subsequently revalued on a full commercial basis at £210,000 – a 10% uplift in just four years.

Use vendor finance and lease options

If you get to the vendor directly, that opens the door to doing creative deals because you can uncover the seller's motivation. For example, if they don't need the money from the sale, you could discuss what might be the best solution for them. Perhaps you could agree on either of the following.

Buy, then lend

You buy the property now, and have them lend you the money back at an agreed interest rate. They get a guaranteed sale and monthly rental income for a fixed period of time, while you don't need money upfront to purchase it. When the property rises in value, after the works or over time, you can refinance it to repay the vendor.

Purchase lease option

You lease the property from them with a fixed purchase price at the end, another no-money-down strategy, because the rent you agree to pay comes from tenants. This gives you the option to buy the property but obliges the vendor to sell it to you only when you are ready to buy.

If the numbers work, you could even offer more than the property is currently worth, if you're confident that you can uplift the future value sufficiently – so that when you do buy it, it will still be a good deal. In the meantime, you have enjoyed income from the property, and the owner receives a rental payment every month.

This can work well for existing HMOs that need some love and attention, where the vendor is not yet ready to let go of the income. Take control of the rent, renovate the property and take the uplift in rent that you achieve as your profit.

Leverage online tools

I seriously can't imagine doing property investing and developing without the internet. Before that, buyers had to get out of bed and leave the house! Those old enough will remember the occasional flyovers from a local pilot, who then sold the aerial shots. Nowadays, all we need is a screenshot courtesy of Google Earth.

This enables us to view a property from above, beside it, in 3D, and even take a virtual walk around the neighbourhood via Street View. It's an amazing tool, well worth learning how to use. We use Google Earth to work out where the access is to a property, where we would put bikes and bins, and whether the loft is high enough to convert.

We can also use it to spot the odd one out. If we know an area is in tenant demand, we can search for properties to see which haven't yet been extended or converted. We use it to look for properties that are in the wrong location: for example, offices in residential areas. Once we identify properties that work, we can source the property's address, download the title deed from the Land Registry, and approach the owner directly to see if they're looking to sell, now or in the near future.

Alternatively, we can use a tool which has all of this information in one place. Nimbus Maps has been great at reaching out to the property developer community to see what we need. Because it links to Google Earth, we can take a look around and instantly see the address, title plan, flood risk information, listed building data and much more. Essentially, it draws from all the main portals, putting the data in one place and making it user-friendly. You can also search by property type, eg office or retail.

One great feature of Nimbus is its ability to search for HMOs that will work within the planning policy: 10% of HMOs within a 50-m radius. This helps to save time when looking for opportunities in an Article 4 area.

Leverage sourcing agents

Using sourcing agents can be a great time saver, but not all sourcing agents are the same. Some will do no more than direct you to a link on Rightmove and say they've got it for asking price. Does that sound like great service? Most would probably charge a bit to provide a service: for example, a better deal, a direct-to-vendor deal or to secure a below market-value deal. Also, the way your sourcing agent works out the numbers might be totally different to how you calculate them, so always double check their numbers to ensure they work for you

All that aside, some sourcing agents are fantastic, and will get you some mega-deals.

TOP TIP

Hand them your hunting brief. Never hand over non-refundable money. Verify numbers, Gross Development Value (GDV) and comparables.

Finally, view the property yourself.

Now you know where to find the deals, it's time to talk about what to do when you find one.

PART FOUR
REVIEW AND DELIVER

12
Analysing HMO Deals

G etting this right is definitely an artform: it's where profits are made and lost, so we have structured our method to reflect this. ART covers the three main points:

- Analyse

- Raise the funding you need to leverage your resources

- Team – build the greatest one possible

Up to this point, we have worked on the D and the A of the DNA of a Next Level HMO®, now to fill in the blank and see if the numbers work (Figure 12.1).

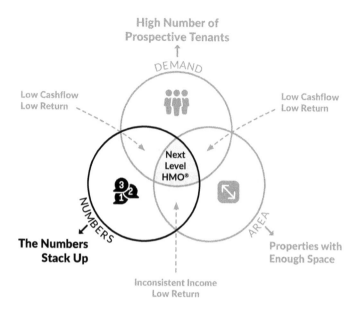

High Number of
Prospective Tenants

DEMAND

Low Cashflow
Low Return

Low Cashflow
Low Return

Next
Level
HMO®

NUMBERS

AREA

**The Numbers
Stack Up**

Properties with
Enough Space

Inconsistent Income
Low Return

Figure 12.1: The DNA of a Next Level HMO® – the numbers

I like numbers. For some though, they are another language entirely. If that sounds like you, before you run for the hills, my goal is to make this part as straightforward as possible. If you find you're still struggling, don't give up yet. Crunching the numbers is easily outsourced either to a professional, or a potential partner whose strengths complement yours.

Yield versus return

'Yield' is a widely used term in the property industry, but it means different things to different people. As investors, we do not normally weigh yield as a key factor. Instead, return on cash invested (ROCI) is our focus.

That said, when working out a project's end value – its Gross Development Value (GDV) – yield becomes an important number. We'll look at calculating GDV for commercial HMOs later in this chapter; for now, let's look at the difference between yield and ROCI.

Yield

When used correctly, yield is a gross figure that does not consider any costs, operational or borrowing. The only two things we need to calculate yield are property value and turnover.

$$\text{Yield} = \frac{\text{Annual Turnover}}{\text{Property Value}} \times 100$$

Turnover is how much rent the entire property generates annually, when fully operational. The property value is generally the price paid: the sold price. For the Next Level HMO® strategy, we want to know the comparable sold prices of similar products or properties to what we intend to create.

Return on cash invested

ROCI is calculated by dividing the net annual profit (ie, annual profit after all running, management and borrowing costs) by the amount of cash that you, as the developer, will use or have used, to purchase and improve the property:

$$ROCI = \frac{Net\ Annual\ Profit}{Cash\ Invested} \times 100$$

ROCI is slightly more difficult to calculate because it involves a number of factors. As long as you keep your methodology consistent, you can use this to gauge how different projects compare with each other. It also tells you how much cash is in each project and how hard it will work, or is working, for you. It's a key indicator of whether or not a deal is a 'goer'.

Deal analysis

As well as ROCI, we need to know what we can afford to pay for the property. The fundamental piece of information is how much the project will be worth when it's finished.

TOP TIP

Start every project with the end in mind.

We can work backwards from there, using a simple formula to calculate what our maximum offer should be:

End Value – Profit – Cost of Works – Cost of Finance – Cost of Purchase = Maximum Offer

End value

The end value, or GDV, of our project is likely to be the commercial value. There are a lot of misconceptions around what a commercial valuation is. I hear this a lot: 'How do you work out a commercial valuation?', 'Can I get a commercial valuation on this?'

Commercial valuations are seen as the holy grail, and people assume they are far higher than the bricks-and-mortar value. (Bricks-and-mortar value means that if the property doesn't pass tests of planning or extensive works, it will be valued as the resale value as if it were any other property in the street.)

When does a property qualify for a commercial valuation? To know this, we need to think like a bank. How would they view it if they needed to get their money back and repossess the property?

TOP TIP

If your property can easily be sold as a family home, it's ineligible for a commercial valuation.

When I started out, I was told that you could get a commercial valuation on any HMO property. But once I attempted to get these valuations, I discovered this wasn't true. Your property may have a premium if it falls within certain criteria, but the smaller the property, and the more like a family home it is, the less likely that it's the case. In fact, it's a key criterion.

If you were hoping to hedge your bets and use this as an exit strategy, it won't work. You have to be all in, and commit: make it a commercial HMO, and commit to selling it as a commercial HMO.

Note that in some areas, bricks-and-mortar values are actually higher than the commercial value, so it is not a one-size-fits-all proposition. This is where the confusion lies. A property is likely to get a commercial valuation when it is no longer economical to be converted to a house. If it has undergone extensive works, and the costs to put it back to a house are prohibitive, the likely purchaser will not be a family. This type of property may have more than one kitchen or en-suites in every room.

Assuming the above criteria are met, there are three ways to all but guarantee a commercial valuation for a property. They are done with planning permission, and only if you have crossed a planning barrier through historic 'grandfather' rights (where the property is already in use as an HMO before an Article 4 directive came in) or a new, successful application:

- *Sui generis* planning permission – for more than seven unconnected people to live at the property

- C4 permission in an Article 4 area – for between three and six people to live at the property

- A commercial element to the property – residential and commercial use on one legal title, and one loan; the bank will look at the turnover of the entire property

These three are not easy to do, so the bank views them as having value: they are more likely to be sold to an investor than a homeowner. If your property ticks the box of being difficult to convert back but hasn't passed a planning hurdle, you can still get the bank to value your property at a premium. But it won't be the full commercial value that you are looking for; rather, a hybrid valuation. This mainly applies where you have a C4 HMO in a non-Article 4 area.

HYBRID VALUATION

We purchased a property for £105,000 in Warrington. We spent just under £65,000 to convert it to a five-bed, five-en-suite HMO with a communal kitchen/diner. If this property were a family home, it would be valued around £140,000; but as a commercial HMO, it is now worth £170,000.

We uplifted the value, but not by as much as we would have done if it were a full commercial valuation. This is the hybrid valuation where the valuer considers that the property has had extensive works done to create the HMO, and it would cost more to put the property back to being a home than it is worth.

Only certain banks will do this, so it pays dividends
to have a great broker on board who can look at the
situation and advise the right bank for you.

The amount of uplift you get from the bank will
depend on the valuer on the day; but as a general
rule, it will be the purchase price plus costs of works.
Anyone can buy the house next door, spend the same
amount of money on it and create the same product –
so why would they pay a full commercial value for it?

Now we know this, ideally, we want to aim for a high
commercial value. There are two ways to calculate
this, and fundamentally they do the same thing. For
each way, there are three variables: rent, property
value and local yield or multiplier.

The first and easiest way is based on the multiplier for
HMOs in your area:

$$GDV = \text{Gross Rent} \times \text{Comparable Multiplier}$$

The gross (total) rent is the turnover of the property as
if it is full. Next, work out the comparable multiplier
from other properties that have sold:

$$\text{Comparable Multiplier} = \frac{\text{Property Value (of a sold HMO)}}{\text{Gross Rent}}$$

Ideally, find three sold properties in the past six months, and take the average. This gives the average multiplier to use to calculate the GDV.

This is a pretty simplistic way of working out the GDV, and most valuers will take more into account. Let's take a look at the other method.

This time, we're going to use the local yield to calculate property value:

$$GDV = \frac{\text{Gross Rent}}{\text{Local Yield}}$$

For example, if your seven-bed HMO nearby turns over £30,000, and the local yield of other sold HMOs is 10%, your property would be worth:

30,000 ÷ 10% = £300,000

To operate any business, generally you will have some costs of sale directly related to providing that service. All HMOs have bills for electricity, gas, water, internet, council tax, etc, and it would not be possible to charge rent on the property without these costs being met. The valuer may use net figures after these costs have been deducted, to calculate the true profit.

Most valuers will estimate running costs between 15 and 25% of the rent, depending on where the property is in the country, and how risk-averse the valuer is.

This means that most valuers will use this equation to work out GDV:

$$GDV = \frac{\text{Net Adjusted Rent}}{\text{Net Local Yield}}$$

Using these formulae means that something counter-intuitive can happen. The lower the yield, the higher the end value. For example, on our example property that turns over £30,000 per year, if the yield was lower, say 8%, this means that the value has increased to £375,000. Comparatively, if the yield was higher, say 12%, then the value has decreased to £250,000. We can see how important it is to find out and use the correct yield!

When creating a Next Level HMO®, the two things we want are *high* rental values and *low* yields: this creates a *high* GDV. This does happen because rents and property values do not increase at the same rate as each other. The average room rental is just under £600 per month, and there are rooms to rent at this level in both the north-west and south-east England, but properties transact at extremely varying levels.

Getting certainty on end values is the difficult task. The thing to remember is that GDVs come from comparable properties: it depends on the recent sold prices of similar assets. These would be HMOs and blocks of flats, which can be used by the valuer to hang their hat on.

To get certainty, find the comparables by speaking to estate agents and other landlords who have had valuations, and ask them nicely for a copy of their valuation. Finally, if in any doubt, pay for a commercial valuer to go and value it before you buy. All of this information is invaluable, and I would always suggest that when a valuer surveys your property, you provide them with all the corroborating evidence you can find that supports your estimations in a valuation information pack.

To calculate estimated turnover when analysing a deal, how many rooms are you planning to let? Ideally, you will have reverse-engineered this into your hunting brief; but if you find yourself staring at a floor plan and not knowing where to start, run these high-level numbers.

- How much space do you want per room – eg 11 m²

- How much bathroom space do you want per room – eg 3 m² for an en-suite

- How much communal space do you want per person – eg 4 m² per person

- This will give you a total amount of required space per person – eg 18 m²

- Account for circulation space (corridors, stairs, etc) at 10–15% of the total area

Let's look at an example.

For a 500 m² office building, subtract 15% for circulation space = 425 m²

Total amount of space per person = 18 m²

425 ÷ 18 = 23 bedrooms

Now go to your design team and ask them to find them! Your main hurdle will be finding 23+ windows.

Profit

Obviously, profit is what we are looking to make in our property projects. Normally, we calculate the profit we want as a percentage of GDV.

For example, if we are looking to make 10% profit, it would be calculated as 10% of the GDV. If the GDV is £1 million, the profit would be £100,000. Still, 10% is not high enough profit to get lending from institutions: usually they want to see 20% of GDV as profit – so in this example, it would be £200,000 of the £1 million project.

If we are looking to pull all our money out, we would aim for 25% profit. This is because at the end of the project, we are going to refinance and the maximum commercial loan available at the time of writing is 75% loan-to-value (LTV). In this £1 million project, the loan from a bank is going to be 75% of GDV, so £750,000. To pull out all of the money that has been invested in the project, we have to be able to pay it all off with the 75% loan. When we appraise, we would start by subtracting a profit of 25%.

Cost of works

Cost of works is where most people start to become frustrated, as they struggle to pin it down. Once you have done a few in your area, then you know; but at the beginning, we are looking for a worst-case scenario.

Normally, you can calculate a price per square-foot rate for conversion projects and new-build elements, then the total build cost accordingly. If there are any identifiable extra costs, such as installing new utilities, add that on top. Once you have the final number, include an amount for professional fees. For smaller projects, this could be up to 15% of the build cost, going down to 12% as the costs get larger.

Next, include the all-important contingency. If you are confident with your numbers then use 10% contingency; if you are risk-averse, use 15–20%. There is an argument that until the project has been ripped out, you don't know what you're going to find. Unforeseen costs are inevitable and to be expected on top of what the builder quotes – so be sure to allow for this.

Always sense-check your estimates:

- Get builders' estimates (we do this every time, before we offer on any project)

- Submit some plans to an online estimation service (eg estimators-online.com) for a breakdown of costs

- Speak to a quantity surveyor and engage one, if you see the value (it may be overkill, depending on the scale of your project)

- Track your build costs as you go, to calculate the price per square-foot that you achieve

Cost of finance

Since developers usually borrow money to do the works and buy the building, always factor in 10% on top of all costs to cover borrowing. Even if you use your own money, factoring in 10% allows you some flexibility to use institutional finance, if needed. (Note that by using your own cash or doing a joint venture, this cost can be removed from your appraisal.)

Cost of purchase and maximum offer

We now consider the fees associated with the purchase and any stamp duty. Let's look at an example of an appraisal of a commercial property.

GDV	£1,000,000.00
Profit (25% of GDV)	-£250,000.00
Estimated cost of works	£-300,000.00
Cost of finance for works (at 10% interest)	-£30,000.00
Subtotal	**£420,000.00**
Cost of finance for the purchase (at 10% interest)	£42,000.00
Cost of purchase (solicitors and disbursements, etc)	-£8,000.00
Subtotal (pre-stamp duty)	**£370,000**
Commercial stamp duty	-£8,000.00
Maximum offer	**£362,000.00**

This is the maximum offer before Stamp Duty Land Tax has been calculated. We then work out stamp duty on this amount, which gives us a conservative and final maximum offer.

The commercial stamp duty in this example is £8,000, which leaves us with a maximum offer of £362,000.

Income analysis

We now know what we can offer for the property, but is it worth it for the income? This is the next step. When analysing a property deal, apply these rules (Table 12.1).

Table 12.1: *Income analysis calculation (per month)*

Gross rent	Assume all rooms full
−Mortgage interest	use 6% annual interest
−Management	use 15% of the gross rent
−Bills (conservative)	use £100 per tenant
−Maintenance allowance	use 5–10% (refurb, depending)
=Cash flow	Profit

Take the gross rent assuming that all rooms are full, then subtract all the holding and running costs of the property.

- **Mortgage:** Take 75% LTV of the GDV and calculate the monthly interest-only mortgage payment using a 6% interest rate. This will give you a conservative number for the mortgage; it also builds in some contingency and the ability for the interest to vary.

- **Management:** Even if you self-manage, include an amount here to account for your time or someone else's, which has a value. A figure of around 15% is what you should be paying for an HMO letting agent, taking any extras fees into account.

- **Bills:** £100 per tenant per month is a conservative estimate. As you get more tenants into a property, you might be able to bring this number down per head with economy of scale.

- **Maintenance:** In designing good-looking properties that you want to keep in a good and relettable condition, you may want to repaint between tenancies and implement a proactive maintenance schedule. If you have refurbished the property recently, a 5% maintenance budget should suffice; if not, allow for a 10% maintenance budget. This is money to be put to one side every month, without fail.

- **Voids:** Voids are somewhat inevitable, even if it's just a couple of days between tenancies. It can be covered in the overestimated amounts above, but you may want to include a line in your calculation for it.

- **Furniture leasing:** This is tax-efficient but expensive. It means offsetting the entirety of the lease payment against income to reduce taxable profits. Chat with your accountant to discuss leasing options.

Revisiting return on cash invested

Now we've got a maximum offer and know how much cash we need to be able to buy the deal. But how hard is the money going to work for us in the future?

As we've seen, the ROCI formula is generally worked out from how much cash is left in the deal after works are complete and refinancing. If you have chosen to find deals that pull all the cash out, this will be an infinite return on cash, but you might be happy with

15–20% ROCI. Ultimately the choice is yours – the lower the return you need to achieve, the more deals will work for you.

How to structure an offer

Once you've found something that works for you in terms of location, size and price, it's time to offer. By this stage, you will have worked out your maximum offer based on turnover and yield, as well as your target ROCI. That should never be your first offer – you want room to negotiate, to work up to it gradually, in the hope of getting a deal in the process.

The 'round–round–random' method

This offer method is one that many developers use, calculating all three offers before making the first one:

- Offer #1 – round number, farthest away from the asking price

- Offer #2 – round number, the midpoint between your first offer and your maximum offer price

- Offer #3 – random number at your maximum offer price – just pick random versus whole numbers

When you frame this final offer to the agent or the vendor, say that you have rerun your numbers and have pushed everything to the max to eke out every penny. Once the offer has gone in, don't make any further offers; if you do, you'll have lost faith with both agent and vendor.

Hold fast

Stick at it. It may take three or six months or longer before it comes back to you – there's always a chance, especially if it's a commercial deal, because more than half of commercial deals fail. Bottom line: if the vendor has tried and failed once or twice, they're likely to be desperate to get rid of the property, and either willing to move on price or to work with you to do the deal.

Don't be afraid to go low! Often, a commercial building is priced higher initially to gauge demand: eg £600,000, before selling for much lower – eg £400,000.

Offer conditions

We can and should offer subject to certain caveats. The top three are:

- Structural survey

- Supplying a VAT1614D certificate

- Planning permission

Structural survey

A survey helps ensure you're not going to encounter major structural works beyond your original scope.

VAT

If the property is a commercial property, check if VAT is payable on the sale. The vendor may have opted to tax the building, which means VAT would be payable. If you intend to develop then sell, you can get that back at the end of the project; but if you intend to keep it, that's money out of your pocket forever.

To get around this, you need the vendor to sign VAT form VAT1614D prior to exchange, which disallows VAT on the sale if the property is being converted to residential.

Planning permission

If you don't yet have all the permissions you need to do the works, you can offer Subject to Planning, which gives you time to submit everything you need. Why would a vendor agree to this? If their property has been stuck on the market, or they've had a few sales fall through, they might be willing to work with your solution. Alternatively, you might be able to offer more than your competition, once planning is in place.

To protect yourself, you can get an exclusivity agreement drawn up between you and the vendor to ensure they can't sell to anyone else for a reasonable period of time while the planning application is being considered.

You can also exchange Subject to Planning, as this creates a more binding contract: one that neither side can pull out of, unless planning is refused. This can save you money, and mitigate risk. If you own the property and have it on finance, you will be paying to hold the building, which is pointless and expensive.

Analysing multiple deals can be time consuming, which is why to take this high-level approach. It means that you can look at floor plans, use a rule of thumb to calculate the number of rooms, then use a few variables to calculate if the project is worth diving into detail.

Once you decide that a project is worth taking further, analyse it in detail, get quotes from your team and put in your offer. In England and Wales, offers are not binding until exchange, so you have time to continue due diligence, once that offer has been accepted.

The most important first step is to get that deal into your control.

13
Raising Funding

Do you believe you can raise finance? This can be a major hurdle for many: not in terms of the difficulty in doing it, but belief in yourself. If you don't believe you can raise money to do this business, then you won't.

Should you use your own money first, to put your money where your mouth is? We didn't have that luxury, not having money when we got started; so we had to tackle raising finance from day one – and I'm glad we did.

Most of us have been engrained to believe that somehow, borrowing money is bad. But it's only bad if it's done irresponsibly – without a concrete, viable plan to repay it. If you view borrowing as bad, that's a huge obstacle to becoming a successful business owner (unless you have unlimited personal funds), because the ability to borrow is the lifeblood of most businesses, especially in property. Borrowing permits us to leverage what we do have and create more assets with it.

If the idea of borrowing makes you queasy, the first thing you need to do is to alter your thinking.

Where's the money?

There is an abundance of money out there, and your job as a developer, is to work out how to funnel it to you.

We have identified eight sources of funding that work for HMOs, divided into three types:

- Institutional funding (commercial financing)
- Crowdfunding
- Private funding

Generally, a combination of these three types is used to put a deal together, depending on the length of time for which you need the finance. Figure 13.1 shows how you might fund an HMO development from beginning to end.

Figure 13:1: The HMO funding process

As all good developers do, when we think about finance we start with the end in mind: identify the exit lender that will provide the long-term loan product, then work backwards through the various funding source options.

TOP TIP

Maximise your loan level from financial institutions, as you can leverage this most.

Types of finance

Standard HMO mortgage

This type of lending is available to anyone: currently, no landlord or property experience is required to qualify for a basic HMO mortgage. A standard HMO mortgage is based on bricks-and-mortar value, so there is no premium attached to a property being an HMO.

If you have done substantial works to the property, this type of lender may even value the property lower than you anticipate, because they consider the cost required to revert the property to a single-family home. (This is a rarity, but it depends on how each bank views HMOs.)

The great thing about a standard HMO mortgage is that the interest rate is a lot lower than commercial rates: around the 3–4% per annum mark for 75% loan-to-value (LTV). You can obtain a higher LTV as some will lend up to 85%, and finance for up to 35 years on an interest-only basis.

Commercial HMO mortgage

Commercial banks view such property differently: they see it as a business and consider rental turnover *when* calculating its value. This is the commercial-style valuation that we looked at in Chapter 12 on HMO analysis. Banks that offer commercial mortgages have differing criteria, so if you intend to use a commercial bank as your exit lender, speak to them *before* the project begins, to ensure you'll qualify.

Currently, there is a maximum 75% LTV available through most of these banks, while other lenders generally do lower LTVs. Typically, interest rates range between 4% and 7%, depending on the project. Some banks may insist on shorter terms (for example, one we use offers ten-year terms).

Despite higher rates and shorter terms, if you tick the boxes for this lending type, these banks provide maximum value at the end of your project.

Bridging finance

Bridging is the best way to purchase property quickly. Compared with a mortgage, there is generally less due diligence done on you, the deal and the property, because lenders can use insurance, such as search indemnity, to cover themselves, making it a quick way to transact. As such, bridging is ideal to give you negotiating power or to buy at auction. Naturally, this factors into their return, so you will pay as much as 7–15% per annum plus fees, which can be serviced monthly or deducted from the loan at the beginning.

Banks offer bridging options, which can be quite attractive compared with companies solely offering bridging finance. If you go to a bank for bridging finance, expect more due diligence done on everything, taking more time and erasing the speed advantage.

A true bridging lender moves faster, is more flexible, will be more creative and lend towards property value, *not* the purchase price. Why is that important? Because if you secure a deal below market value, you can borrow more of the purchase price.

Here is a comparison between the two bridging types.

Property value: £100,000, purchase price: £75,000

- Standard bank: LTV = 75% of purchase price or £56,250; 25% cash deposit required = £18,750 plus purchase costs

- Bridging lender: LTV = 75% of property value or £75,000; cash required = £0, plus purchase costs

Congratulations! You've just bought a deal with no money down.

Bear in mind that when you use a bridging loan, you still need to cover refurbishment costs because you have used the first charge of the property to purchase the property, rather than develop it. Still, there are other options.

Bridge-to-let

This is an interesting mortgage product which can work well for smaller HMOs, especially because it's a cheaper form of bridge. Essentially, it's a halfway house between bridging and development finance – meaning the bank finances some of the costs towards the works above what they would normally lend.

In doing this, you work with one bank from initial purchase through to refinance, telling them your full plans and giving them your schedule of works for the project. They value the property at its current value, assess your works, and calculate the future value on completion. This means you know exactly what your property will be worth when finished, before you start. You pay one set of fees, one valuation, and experience a far quicker and smoother transition to your long-term loan.

This type of product works for small HMOs, small conversions and house-to-flat conversions. For our purposes, the caveat is that it's only available for HMOs with a maximum of six lettable rooms. Smaller deals are where you can benefit, perhaps using this for improving existing HMOs inside an Article 4 area.

Development finance

Development finance turns a mortgage on its head and adheres to a main principle of this book: start with the end in mind. Let's first explore how banks view risk, and the levels of security that you can provide.

First charge

This is the maximum security that a bank can be granted. The first charge lender has control over everything. If the project goes wrong and the bank has to come in and finish or sell, it determines what happens with the money.

Second charge

Second in the pecking order, this is not as valuable as a first charge. If something goes wrong, the second charge lender has to wait until the first charge lender has done their bit to sell the property and recoup their investment. Only then, if there is any money left over, does the second charge lender recover part or all of their costs.

Importantly, the first charge lender doesn't have to make sure that there is enough money left for the second charge lender. They can elect to sell the property cheaply to secure a quick deal, at a price just high enough to recover their own costs.

How to structure a development finance deal

This time, instead of looking at how much we need to buy the property, we consider the total amount that we need to do the deal: to cover the purchase and the planned development. We want to borrow as much as possible towards the total cost to reduce the amount of cash required from us.

Most lenders will go up to 80% of total costs, others as much as 85% or even 90%, assuming the numbers make it worth their while.

Begin by working back from the Gross Development Value (GDV). How much profit margin do you anticipate? This must be a minimum of 18–20% to get any lending whatsoever; banks won't lend without it.

Now, look at the costs. Tally all the refurbishment costs, and include any and all professional fees and contingency that you have chosen. Add to that the purchase price and any associated costs to get the total. Most development lenders will lend at least 70% of this total cost, the majority of those even lending up to 80%. They are considered to be your primary lender, and take the first charge.

We've still got a second charge left to play with: mezzanine finance lenders can come in and top up to 90% of costs by way of the second charge. As they are behind the first charge lender in the pecking order, this is understandably more expensive. This leaves only 10% cash required by you, your joint venture partner or investor (Figure 13.2).

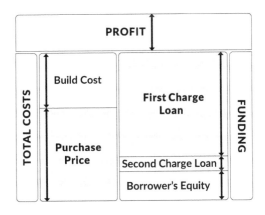

Figure 13.2: Development financing model

Note that the percentages vary, depending on the lender and their criteria. They will also take into account the interest that you pay, and have lending limits against the GDV as well as the cost. While not quite as simple as portrayed above, this should help demystify the concept.

When using development finance to receive your funds linked to the works, the bank will send a monitoring surveyor to check and sign off the works before release of funds. Bear in mind that this comes with an extra cost that we have to bear.

Crowdfunding

Traditionally, financing a business, project or venture involved asking one or a few parties for sizeable sums of money. Crowdfunding reverses this, using the internet to solicit modest amounts from hundreds, thousands, sometimes even millions of potential funders. How does it work?

There are two types of crowdfunding for property:

- Peer-to-peer – people lend a sum of money to fund a property project at a fixed interest rate of generally 7–12% per annum

- Equity funding – people buy shares in a property project

In equity funding, people are given the projected returns and must make an informed decision about whether to invest. They will benefit in a share of the profit, but if the project overruns or the market declines, the profit for both the investor and developer will decrease (Figure 13.3).

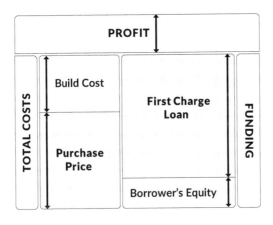

Figure 13.3: Crowdfunding investment model

Crowdfunding works similarly to the development finance model. Investors underwrite the purchase and refurbishment and/or build of your project. If you go with peer-to-peer lending, you will have to put in your cash as the equity share. If you do an equity-style development, you could use crowdfunding for a project without using any of your own cash, by giving shares in your company to your investors.

How to choose crowdfunding finance

Having become popular, crowdfunding is now a more regulated sector in the finance industry. There are good and not so good platforms, so how do we pick the right one for our project?

- Start with their website, and call them. Most are small businesses and, unlike the banks, often you can speak with a decision-maker quite easily.

- What returns do they offer investors? You want your deal to attract investors.

- What security might they require? Some, not all, require charges on the property.

- How much property experience must you possess? While some insist that you be an experienced developer, others are happy simply to vet your team.

- Do they require planning permission in place? Some do, while others let you use their platform to raise funds for speculative planning gain projects.

- How do they update their investors? Perhaps invest a little into the platform to see what their lender experience is like.

Crowdfunding is generally more flexible, more personal and regulated by the Financial Conduct Authority – so you can advertise your deal until you're blue in the face!

Brokers

Finally – and as a prelude to the next chapter – one of the key members of your team is your finance broker. Engage with them when you appraise deals, and discuss the endgame: who is your target lender at the end of the project? Once you can answer that question, you will know where to start.

Bear in mind that brokers vary greatly in experience, knowledge and quality. You are looking for a commercial broker with experience with commercial banks.

Qualifying questions to ask a broker:

- Do you invest in property yourself?

- How many transactions do you do per month?

- With whom? [name of bank]

- What is your specialism?

- Are you regulated by the Financial Conduct Authority?

When you find a good one, hold onto them: the person you want will be a creative thinker to solve problems. Avoid anyone who constantly throws problems at you.

Let's explore the rest of the team you need.

14
Build Your Team And Check Their Knowledge

What is your skill set: are you in construction? Have you had any property experience? Are you a numbers or people person? Whatever your skill set, inevitably there will be gaps you cannot fill amid all of the qualities needed in your team, especially if you have no or limited experience in property.

This industry is all about the team, not the individual. One key task is to build up a reliable team which can perform consistently, long-term, as weak links cost you time and money. It may take some time to build one that's strong, reliable and consistent.

That said, team members are living, breathing creatures, and even a solid group can start to fray at the edges. Accept that part of your responsibility is to periodically reassess, reinvigorate and replace, if need be. A good team is an investment: it's money upfront which may feel like it hurts to spend it, but as the old saying goes, 'buy cheap, buy twice'.

The same is true of your team – get and pay for the right one.

We have had situations where a good builder is great for three projects, but drops the ball on the fourth. Or a letting agent is great for two years until a key staff member leaves, and service subsequently drops. These things happen, so expect them. Again, when you find someone good, hold onto them – but never grow complacent.

What constitutes a power team? Let's look at who you need, when you need them and why.

Your power team

Project manager

This person is your eyes and ears. They work as an independent liaison between you and the contractor, providing on-site supervision on a weekly or fortnightly basis. They cost money but pay for themselves over the long run between saving you money and ensuring the build is good quality.

If you are focused on one project at a time and live close to it, you might save money by donning that cap yourself; but if you have limited build knowledge, the experience that a construction specialist project manager brings is invaluable. By being dedicated to you, there is freedom to run two or more projects consecutively.

The project manager runs the tendering process and arranges the build contract. Sometimes called a contract administrator, whose skill set might be as an architect or a surveyor, these are construction specialists who are familiar with the happenings on a building site. Their role is to sign off on the progress of the works, ensuring they are done to agreed specifications.

They also serve between you and the builder or contractor as an independent arbiter in making payments, to keep the build going while ensuring the builder is never overpaid. Be sure to engage a project manager first.

Architect

Your architect should be registered with the Architects Registration Board in the UK. They are also likely to be a member of a professional body, such as the Royal Institute of British Architects (RIBA).

When working on HMOs, it is essential to get an architect who understands the pertinent building regulations and HMO licensing, to ensure they incorporate the correct requirements from day one, as well as your business and the branding requirements that you've identified from your local tenant research. Plans are recommended for building regulations, and most Next Level HMOs require some element of planning – so you will need plans drawn up and amended as appropriate.

For example, when we find a potential deal, we review it with our architect, citing the minimum number of rooms we want to achieve in the project. This is a quick overview based on our initial thoughts: if the architect agrees, we immediately instruct a measured survey of the property to get rolling on the project's design.

Architects are key throughout the build: they should be on hand to make any changes to plans that the building might throw up when works start. You can try to be as accurate as possible but plans will always need to change, if only slightly.

Interior designer

A designer helps to maximise long-term returns, as superior design commands higher rents and increased tenant satisfaction and longevity. Bringing in an interior designer at the design stage alongside your architect means that you can maximise the property not only for space but functionality, useability and long-term appeal.

For example, we ask our interior designer to examine the history of the property and the area, and to incorporate that into the design. They also do a competitor analysis, looking at the other HMOs on the market, noting design pluses and minuses. To stand out among our competitors, we need to be different, preferable: this includes avoiding the kinds of furniture packs, grey feature walls or other cookie-cutter decor echoed in the majority of HMOs.

Structural engineer

The structural engineer does exactly what it says on the tin: removing or moving walls, adding dormers, tanking basements – all of this requires structural calculations to create a safe and solid end result. The engineer works with your architect to design any required alterations into the plans and, ideally, saves you money by suggesting cost-effective solutions that retain the structural integrity of the building.

SAP consultant

The Standard Assessment Procedure (SAP) is the methodology used by the Government to assess and compare the energy and environmental performance of new dwellings.[21] If you're converting a commercial building into residential, you will require a SAP report and Energy Performance Certificates (EPCs)[22] to be created.

Get this done early based on your proposed specification of works, because it can be expensive to rectify issues if you overlook something, or your scheme misses the necessary 'E' rating to let the property.

Builder

While you may think the builder is the most important member of your team, lining up the right team of project manager, architect, interior designer and structural engineer leads to finding a good builder. They may have good contacts that they have used successfully in the past.

How to tender

The tendering process is where you furnish the detailed schedule of works and construction plans to builders or contractors, who then bid for the work. Be sure to request bids from three to five firms, to keep things competitive. Construction drawings typically

---

21 'Standard Assessment Procedure' (Department for Business, Energy & Industrial Strategy, 2013, updated 2014), www.gov.uk/guidance/standard-assessment-procedure, accessed 11 November 2020

22 'Guide to Energy Performance Certificates' (Energy Saving Trust, no date), https://energysavingtrust.org.uk/advice/guide-to-energy-performance-certificates-epcs, accessed 11 November 2020

include structural alterations as noted by the structural engineer and architect, and the schedule of works is designed in spreadsheet format with line items listed, so the builder merely fills in the blanks for each list item.

Your schedule of works is a key communication tool: a document that can be referred to at any time during the build, the level of detail driven by who assembles it and who is being asked to quote. You can create this yourself by popping to a DIY store and listing all the items you want in the property, from fire doors to taps, or have your project manager or architect do this for you.

The tendering process begins with a site visit by potential builders, who are given a deadline of normally one to three weeks to assemble a quote. You want to ensure the quotes you receive are for comparable work. (Recently, we were given three quotes, one being considerably cheaper. Closer examination revealed the inexpensive quote didn't include doors or windows despite being in the scope of work.)

When you're considering builders, view their previous jobs, and ask for and check their references. Going cheap isn't necessarily the way to save, and time is a factor in staying on budget. For example, if a builder realises they have underquoted, they may reduce the number of workers as they don't have the cash to pay them, which slows the build down.

The build contract

Once you have chosen the main contractor, your project manager will put together the build contract. This could be as basic as a single sheet of A4 that sets out the obligations and expectations of both parties; but we recommend using a contract such as the ones that the Joint Contracts Tribunal provides.[23] The contract should include a payment schedule and penalties for late completion, and/or incentives for early completion. Also, there should be a retention of funds clause for the rectification of any issues, once completed.

TOP TIP

If you put a contract in front of a builder and they run a mile, they are not a builder you want to use!

VAT

You will likely pay VAT to your builder, and for conversion projects to HMO or flats, this will qualify for the reduced rate of 5% VAT. If you do a refurbishment project, like buying and upgrading an existing HMO, you pay the standard 20% VAT. Your builder should know to charge you the correct VAT. If they are uncertain, refer them to their accountant and VAT Notice 708, Part 7, where it clearly states that 'you may be able to charge VAT at the reduced rate of 5% if you

---

23 www.jctltd.co.uk

are converting premises into a "multiple occupancy dwelling", such as bed-sits'.[24]

Once you have put your team in place, you will want to check their knowledge against a basic understanding of the moving parts of construction.

Building regulations

There is a lot of legislation concerning construction. This is to keep people safe, whether that be tenants, construction workers or us financially. Leverage your team to implement these, but this section includes the basics of which you should always be aware.

Building regulations are divided into parts, called Approved Documents A–R (except I and O), and are designed to provide clear guidelines on everything from the structure through to drainage and windows. Developers must comply with all of these when doing any construction, but it's unlikely you'll deal with every single part.

There are two ways to submit a building regulations application:

---

24 See Paragraph 7.4 of the Buildings and Construction (VAT Notice 708): www.gov.uk/guidance/buildings-and-construction-vat-notice-708#section7.

- Full plans

- A building notice

If you plan to do a minor amount of work, a building notice may suffice. If you plan to do significant works, including lots of en-suites and structural work, full plans may be the best way to go, as it gets your scheme design signed off before you start and can't be rejected later.

Note: You must always give the council 48 hours' notice of commencement of works.

The only complication with developing HMOs is that they are not always specifically referred to in each Approved Document. This means that there is an element of interpretation in terms of how to apply the building regulations. The person who interprets these documents will be your building inspector and you get an element of choice with this.

There are two routes you can take:

- Local authority building control

- An approved inspector

Our preferred approach is to work with an approved inspector. This gives you the freedom to choose whom you would like to work with, and you can interview them before making a selection.

We will ask them about their previous experience working on HMOs and primarily look for a serious approach to fire safety. We will also ask for their view on the scheme in relation to sound testing (Approved Document E). This is a grey area and they need to decide if your development is 'rooms for residential purposes'.[25] This will dictate the level of sound insulation you install and whether you have to pass sound tests to prove it.

HMO fire safety

This is not an area in which to scrimp and save. I recommend reading the Local Authorities Coordinators of Fire Safety (LACORS) Fire Safety Guide.[26] It states that the general principle of fire safety is to:

1. Alert occupants to a fire via a working fire alarm

2. Provide well-lit escape routes to safely exit the building

Be sure to get this right.

There are two ways to describe a fire detection system:

---

25 *Approved Document E: Frequently Asked Questions* (Department for Communities and Local Government, 2016), https://assets. publishing.service.gov.uk/government/uploads/system/uploads/ attachment_data/file/509347/160321_Part_E_FAQ.pdf, accessed 11 November 2020

26 *Housing – Fire Safety: Guidance on fire safety provisions for certain types of existing housing* (LACORS, 2008), www.cieh.org/media/1244/ guidance-on-fire-safety-provisions-for-certain-types-of-existing-housing.pdf, accessed 11 November 2020

- Grades A–F

- Level of coverage, or LD1, LD2 or LD3.

Fire protection for most HMOs falls under Grades A or D.

Grade A

This system is comparable to what you see in office blocks and hotels: a red 'break glass' button to manually activate an alarm. It is mains-powered, interlinked and managed by a control panel. Normally councils request this for properties of three or more storeys, but legally it isn't required until you hit five storeys.[27]

Grade D

This is still mains-powered and interlinked but does not feature manual call points or a control panel; instead, you can install test switches. This is the minimum requirement for an HMO.

Coverage level

Coverage is divided up into three levels or categories, LD1, LD2 and LD3:

---

27 *Housing – Fire Safety: Guidance on fire safety provisions for certain types of existing housing* (LACORS, 2008), www.cieh.org/media/1244/guidance-on-fire-safety-provisions-for-certain-types-of-existing-housing.pdf, accessed 11 November 2020

- LD1 – detectors in escape routes and all rooms

- LD2 – detectors in escape routes and high fire-risk rooms (eg kitchens)

- LD3 – detectors in escape routes only

At Scott Baker Properties, we go overboard and install both Grade A and LD1 in most Next Level HMOs we build, so that there is a fire sounder in every bedroom. This ensures that even the most comatose of tenants wakes up and gets out if the alarm goes off.

Grade A fire alarms should be tested regularly by a qualified person, but all fire alarms should be tested weekly and recorded in a log book.

Escape routes

These should be fire protected for at least up to 30 minutes using FD30 Fire Doors. They should be self-closing, with intumescent strips that expand with heat to stop smoke.

Emergency lighting may be required if the escape route is long and complex. The exit door on the property's exterior must be openable from the inside without a key, ie a thumb-turn lock. There also can be a secondary means of escape, typically through windows or a dedicated fire escape.

Health and safety: construction design and management regulations

Health and safety is everyone's responsibility. Even if you are not regularly on-site, you own the property and are responsible to ensure the health and safety of those on it.

The Construction Industry Training Board (CITB) provides substantial information on Construction Design and Management Regulations 2015 (CDM 2015),[28] with which you should familiarise yourself. Let's look at some of the key facets.

All projects must have:

- Workers that possess suitable skills, knowledge, training and experience
- Contractors who provide appropriate supervision, instruction and information
- A written construction phase plan

In projects where more than one contractor is involved, you are required to:

---

28 www.citb.co.uk/about-citb/partnerships-and-initiatives/
    construction-design-and-management-cdm-regulations

- Appoint a principal designer and principal contractor

- Provide a health and safety file

If the works are scheduled to last longer than thirty working days, with more than twenty workers working simultaneously at any point in the project, or if it exceeds 500 person-days, you must report your project to the Health and Safety Executive (HSE) using Form F10.

There are three basic roles that must be filled:

- Principal contractor – responsible for health and safety on-site

- Principal designer (normally the architect or project manager) – responsible for building in risk management at the design stage

- The client (you)

You or the contractor must provide the following:

- Personal protective equipment (PPE)

- Welfare facilities

- A first-aider on-site

- Insurance in place and up-to-date

- Risk assessment and method statements for the project

New-build warranties

If you do a conversion to flats and intend to sell, you must provide a new-build warranty. New-build warranties protect a property from defects for up to ten years from date of construction; the most well-known is the National House Building Council (NHBC) warranty.[29]

If you intend to convert and hold the property, you must ask your exit lender about their requirements where this is concerned. You always have the option to obtain a Professional Consultant's Certificate, although it is only good for six years versus ten. Any property professional can provide this, including your surveyor, engineer and, more likely, your architect. It is backed by their insurance, so be sure to get a copy.[30]

Party wall agreements

Party walls are boundaries that are jointly owned. If you're following the Next Level HMO® strategy, you're likely to be doing works at the rear or in the loft of your property that will affect a party wall, so it's important to secure party wall agreements and ensure they're done correctly.

The party wall process can be simple or complex and drawn out, depending on the relationship you have

---

29 www.nhbc.co.uk/builders/warranties-and-cover
30 https://lendershandbook.ukfinance.org.uk/lenders-handbook/pcc

with your neighbours. In it, you promise to make good any issues that arise when the work you do on your property affects the neighbouring property.

Note that before you start protesting, this is about fairness. It isn't meant to stop you doing works – and legally, it can't – but worst-case scenario, you need a surveyor to monitor the condition of the neighbouring properties and act as an independent arbiter in case of damage.

You can draw up an agreement yourself (the Government provides templates for this),[31] but if in doubt, engage a party wall surveyor to manage this process for you.

Refurbishment sequence

Once you have bought the property, you want to refurbish it in a sensible order. Your project manager or contractor should take the lead on this process, but let's look at the desired process for those who have never done a major construction project before.

In general, we progress from dirty to clean works and never overlap them, if we can avoid it.

---

31 'Preventing and resolving disputes in relation to party walls' (Ministry of Housing, Communities & Local Government, 2013, updated 2016), www.gov.uk/guidance/party-wall-etc-act-1996-guidance, accessed 11 November 2020

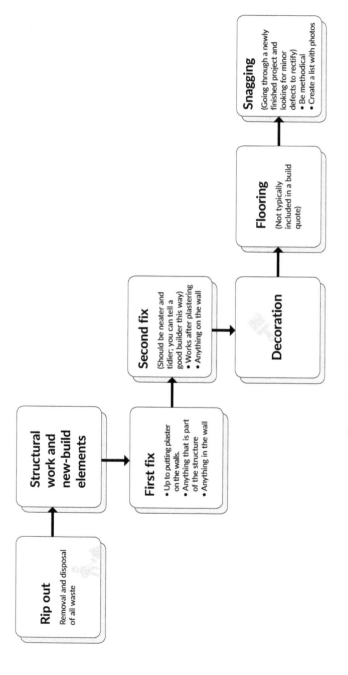

Figure 14.1: The refurbishment process

As you will have gathered, there is a lot to reviewing and delivering projects, and this is where your team comes into its own. Whether you are skilled in some of these areas or not, learn to lean on others and don't be afraid to ask for help. Doing this will take you a lot further than you otherwise would have imagined.

PART FIVE
SERVICE

15
Attracting Prospective Tenants

Reflecting on our opening story in Chapter 1, Niall and I have certainly learned a lot about tenants since then, not just in terms of what to do, but what not to do. You'll recall that despite having created a great HMO, we tripped over the tenant hurdle and in our haste, accepted the first people who applied. We were hungry for the rent!

This is the wrong attitude to have. What we should have been hungry for was the *right* tenant. The right tenant won't cause you issues, will be happy residing in your property, will take pride in it and make it their own.

The Co-living Approach

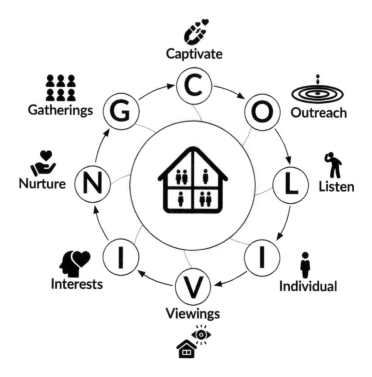

Figure 15.1: The Co-living Approach

How do we attract these tenants to our business and keep them with us? The approach we take we have dubbed the 'Co-living Approach'. This comprises eight elements that, when all included in your modus operandi, will ensure your high-value customers turn up and stay. As mentioned previously, we believe that co-living as a concept is all about the customer experience, so rule number one: stop calling your tenants 'tenants'! The landlord–tenant relationship is such an outdated modus operandi. The focus must turn to a customer-led approach, which means a service-led approach. To help this, we call our tenants 'housemates' or 'customers', and I have seen others use words like 'members', 'residents' or 'sharers'.

All successful businesses aim to provide a level of service that they consistently strive to maintain or surpass. They make a promise and keep it. If you fail to promise a certain level of service, you won't have customers; and if you do make a promise and fail to make good on it, you lose their faith *and* custom. When your disappointed customers tell others, your business quickly disappears.

The Co-living Approach breaks it down for co-living operators or managers.

What promises do we want to make? To answer that, we need to answer this question first: what constitutes good service, not just in property or lettings, but in any type of business? Here are some examples:

- Good communication
- Reliability
- Quick response times
- Accessibility
- Solution-focused
- Organised

- Systematic

- Punctuality

- Knowledgeable

These should link back to your mission, vision and values, and are the tests that you will be applying for potential managing agents.

Let's get into the Co-living Approach.

Captivating your customer

A good business captures the attention and the imagination of its customers. Remember the beige box versus the colourful, mystical, magical iMac in Chapter 2? As mentioned previously, we must create a product which attracts the customers who pay and stay: the top 5% in the marketplace where your HMO is always likely to be fully occupied, because as soon as you drop below this, you fall into the commoditised market where the battle over price begins. The Co-living Approach gives you hints and tips how to get there and stay there.

If you believe that a lot of the other properties – your competitors – out there are worthy of top 5% status, you're not thinking creatively enough. What can you do to stand out: what's your unique selling proposition?

Create your own unique tenant/customer-facing brand and take control of your marketing. Give your house or your property an identity: look into its history to see if there is anything that you can use to help it stand out. Can you even give it a name? When you name it, it is no longer room in a house like everyone else's; it's something different.

FIND THE PROPERTY'S STORY

We bought a property in 2019 whose history, we discovered, was linked to the old local theatre and cinema. The owner had given us a large file of historic papers indicating who had owned it and lived there.

For example, the owners had turned the attic room into a guest suite for touring artists, including George Formby of 'When I'm Cleaning Windows' fame, a hit from the 1936 black and white movie, *Keep Your Seats, Please*. Our designer ran with that theme, right down to featuring a record player in the communal lounge.

How many other HMOs can claim to offer that? (A benefit of having a creative member of your team.)

Once you know your unique selling point, create a website – and potentially social media channels – for the project that focuses on it. Sell the story of the property, its location and any added benefits that the properties next door don't offer. Do this even if you have an agent, because they can use it to boost their marketing on your behalf.

You could even hang your own 'To Let' board, with your URL and contact number, on the outside of the house: you don't have to use the letting agent's branding, but you can still use their number, so you don't have to field calls. The idea here is to think differently.

Advertising your property

First impressions count: this starts with the advert. If you have an agent in place, they should do the majority of the work in advertising for customers; but if you self-manage, you will be hands-on here. Even if you do have an agent, it's always smart to check their work.

As we saw in Chapter 8, the main online forum for advertising rooms for rent is Spareroom.co.uk; but there are many others, including social media. Put yourself in the shoes of your prospective customer: how might they go about finding a room? For example, if you intend to rent to students, it might benefit you to work with the most revered student agency in town, because they get the first pick of tenants without having to advertise online.

Alternatively, you might have an online portal that always works for you – it depends on your market. Try everything to see what sticks. Thinking about how prospective housemates would search for a room to rent, they are most likely to search online for 'room to rent in [town]'. Try that and see what comes up on the first page of your search engine. You want to advertise on all of those sites.

Once you know where to advertise, here's what to put in your advert.

Images and videography

- Photos – have your interior designer stage the property (see Chapter 7), and commission a professional photographer to shoot it.
- Video – commission a professional videographer to film the property. Don't upload a slideshow of stills!

Organise the video shoot for the same day as your photos, so that staging only needs to be done once.

Virtual tour

There are numerous ways of doing a virtual tour. You could video one, or you can use 360-degree scanning with photography technology to create an interactive walkthrough, eg using a tool such as Matterport.

We like 360-degree photographed tours where you can choose what the customer sees: ie only the room that's available, not the entire house.

Amazing copywriting

The key point is to sell the concept and benefits of co-living:

- Living with like-minded people in a community

- A ready-made set of friends and social circle

- The facilities, location, decor and people

- The extra services provided – eg a cleaner for communal areas

- Internet connection, quality and speed – very important

Avoid just three or four bullet points about the property – there needs to be a lot of text here. Some potential housemates only read the first few lines, so those must grab their attention; while others will read every single word and may be impressed by the amount of information. The idea is to appeal to varying styles of people by doing both.

Constructing the advert

- Note the key points in the headline: eg 'large', 'in the city centre', 'co-living', 'bonus savings' – all emphasised by exclamation points.

- For those with short attention spans, use upper-case to grab attention to prime features.

- Imply urgency to act, due to the attractiveness of the offering, but avoid hard selling.

- Expand on the property details for those who read the listing in its entirety, using strong adjectives such as 'stunning', 'magnificent', 'newly refurbished', 'luxury', 'design-led', 'sustainable', 'tech-enabled', etc.

- Sell the location: available transport links, local amenities, furniture, space, facilities and design.

- At the end, summarise the high points.

When you place an ad, it's generally a good idea to include a picture of yourself as a live-out landlord.

Kerb appeal

We've focused on interior design already, but the design of your property starts from the outside:

- What's the first impression visitors have of the building?

- What do they see?

- Does it have kerb appeal?

- What does this say about what might be inside?

Don't forget to focus on the exterior, so that people think 'That's my new home!' when they walk up the road. Anything which can be perceived as negative can give your new customer a niggle in the back of their mind, making them lean towards someone else's property.

Remember where we started: first impressions count.

Outreach

Consider how you can add value beyond letting the rooms. What services can you offer and include in the rent that no other landlord might: for example, could you partner with a local business to deliver a particular service, or perhaps offer a preferred discount to housemates who use the local takeaway, gym, etc? You can provide a service that doesn't cost you anything.

There are providers you can plug into which have connections to larger discounts: they will give your customer discounts, etc. They have done the work for you already, but if you do have time to focus on this more, try reaching out to smaller local businesses which would benefit more from a large influx of local people.

Listen

At the beginning of this chapter, we created a list of qualities that denote good service: the one at the top was good communication – this means listening and responding. Good communication starts before a potential customer has even viewed the property, but must continue well into the operations of letting.

The first item to decide is what forums you want to give customers to communicate with you. Large operators have regular 'town hall' meetings that allow for feedback to be aired in public. They also have a manned customer service desk for resolving issues privately.

On the smaller scale, how could you implement both public and private levels of communication and keep them organised without necessarily having people on-site? A WhatsApp group for the house is a start, but if housemates are communicating about a leaky tap and someone stealing their cheese at the same time, details can get lost.

There are other thread-based systems out there, such as Slack, but my favourite is COHO.life: a tool for HMO and co-living management that puts communication at the heart of its architecture with group messaging, fault reporting and private messaging in one portal.[32]

---

32   https://coho.life

Be reliable

When you have a reliable system, use it effectively. It's all about keeping your promises: do what you say you will and give realistic timescales. When an issue is reported, acknowledge it and let the house-mates know what is being done to fix it and when. Practise under-promising and over-delivering. It goes down better with the housemates to say 'It will be done within 10 days' and is actually done in three, as opposed to saying 'It'll be fixed tomorrow' and it takes a week. That way they'll lose faith in you and are more likely to move out.

If there is a realistic issue in the house, fix it. Don't scrimp and risk annoying your customers. Keep on top of maintenance.

Ask for feedback

Don't always wait for feedback; encourage it and check in with them periodically. When it comes, acknowledge it and let them know that you care. Implement sensible changes and show them that you are always looking to improve the service you provide.

Importantly, always ask departing customers their reasons for leaving. You'd be amazed at just how many landlords and agents fail to do this:

- Is it the property?

- The other housemates?

- The service?

- Are they moving into another HMO in the area – if so, why?

- Are they upgrading to a flat, or moving in with friends?

- Substantially relocating?

If you know why they are choosing to move, you might be able to help them find their next property – ideally one of yours, or that of a friend or colleague.

16
Getting Customers Over The Line

Once the customer is attracted to your business, to get them over the line and into your business, there are two key elements to get right:

- Understanding the needs of the individual
- Conducting a good viewing

So far, this book has talked a lot about community, but it's important to remember that as a landlord we're also dealing with individual needs. When we did our nationwide tenant survey at the beginning of 2020, an overriding fact was that, despite wanting a community to live in, their number one thought was themselves. The space they would inhabit, the communal space they'd have access to and how they'd fit into that community.

Making a potential new housemate feel like they're the most important person, and showing them the life that they can lead, is so important. This allows them to feel at home and take a sense of ownership and belonging. Once they feel this way, they'll integrate and become a part of the community.

Viewing

In this business, viewing is essentially the 'sale'. Once you've captivated prospective customers in your marketing, you need a smooth viewing. There are right and wrong ways to do a sale.

CHECK THE PRESENTATION

A fellow landlord had an agent they were unhappy with, so he sent a friend to go around as a 'mystery shopper'. He reported back that the rooms were only half-dressed, and that the agent said they could have any of the rooms. Also, that there was a flat around the corner they could take which was bigger than his room!

This failed, in that it gave the prospective customer too many options – including a property that wasn't even his!

That led to a quick sacking of the agent.

We need to showcase the positives and create a little scarcity to impress that this room is going to go quickly: if they want it, they need to make a quick decision. It's not a high-pressure sale, but small things can help them make the decision to go with your room rather than the competition. It can mean the difference between someone excitedly wanting to take the room that day, versus leaving to view another five properties.

Here's a formula for an attractive viewing.

Before you show the property, stage the customer's intended bedroom as a showroom: presentation is key.

Dress the bed with extra temporary pillows and an attractive throw or bedspread. (I suggest creating a staging kit for each house and keeping it in a locked cupboard somewhere in the house, maybe under the stairs or in a loft.)

Include ornaments such as a few books, a faux plant or two, candle or vase – things designed to make the space homelier, warmer. The idea is to leave a lasting positive impression of what they're buying, the icing on the cake.

Ensure the entranceway to the property is clear of rubbish. Get there early enough to sweep away any dead leaves or cigarette butts.

Begin the viewing by meeting outside the property to point out local transport links, the closest grocery shops, nearest takeaways, pubs, gym and anything else relevant nearby. Focus on the positives – the amenities that exist – and avoid mentioning those you think they might wish were near but aren't.

Open the door and let them enter ahead of you. If the Wi-Fi router is in the entranceway or on the landing, point it out and impress upon them the internet speed that everyone in the house enjoys. If you know the numbers, eg 300GB per second, then cite this, as it sounds impressive. If you have extenders or other wireless access points throughout the house, point these out to show that being far from the main router doesn't compromise access.

Show them the heating controls, how to turn them on and adjust them. State that bills are included (if this is the case), and that they control the thermostat.

Show the communal facilities first. Begin with the kitchen: their allotted cupboard space, cooking facilities and equipment, dishwasher, washing machine and tumble dryer, then show them the lounge area. If there's a communal TV, indicate any provided channels, such as cable or a house Netflix account. Talk about these services in a caring and service-providing way. As you're walking around the property, mention a little about the existing housemates – what they do, their interests, ages, how many men/women there are and how they socialise. The community is part of the attraction to the property – so don't forget to sell that.

Show them the private bedroom that you've staged. As you explain the benefits, talk about the room as if it's already theirs: eg 'Your room is the quietest in the house, because it's the furthest from the front door', or 'This is the safest room in the house, because it's closest to the front door'.

If the room is en-suite, demonstrate the water pressure by turning on the tap and shower, and say: 'The system has been designed for [X] number of people to shower at once', reassuring them that while they are sharing the property, they won't suffer from low water pressure.

Draw their attention to any available storage: eg under the bed, above the wardrobe, and any built-in storage in the room, en-suite or the property for them to use.

Solicit feedback, don't just leave it to them to decide. Find out what they're thinking, and go for positive reinforcement. Ask them:

- What is your favourite part of the property?

- What is best about the location for you?

- How does this compare to other viewings? (That is, if you're confident that your property is one of the best in town.)

- How could you see yourself living here?

Now do a soft sell:

- 'You'd fit in well here; you'd get along well with the others.'

- 'When can you move in?'

Finally, give them a call to action before they leave, whether they're ready to buy there and then or want some time before deciding.

- For those who are receptive: 'If you want to take the room off the market, then we can get your holding deposit sorted today.' Have a card payment machine ready and paired to your phone to accept payment.

- For those not quite ready, to avoid pushing them away, provide printed information that reinforces the positives, with details of how to reserve the room. (We do this on a postcard that lists property highlights and details on the front, with reservation information on the back.)

An alternative: tenant-led viewings

So far, we've assumed it's the agent or your representative in the area conducting the viewing – but could it be an existing housemate? Could you give them this brief and get them to show the house?

As we've already mentioned, housemates are your best marketing tool, assuming that you are providing the service that you aim to; so why not ask them to show new potential housemates around? They can tell them all about the household and what they get up to, and the existing housemates can even choose their new housemate. How great is that! You know that it will be the best fit.

17
Getting The Right House Dynamic

Speaking of good fit, how do we know that the housemates are going to get on? One way is tenant-led viewings, but another way is to gather data and interview prospective housemates before they move in.

Interviewing potential housemates

Ask them simple questions such as:

- Where do you work?

- What's your salary? (to check affordability)

- Do you have any credit issues?

- Where do you currently live?

- Have you lived in a shared house before?

- Why do you want to live in a shared house?

- What do you know about the area?

- What do you like to do in your spare time?

- Do you follow sport or music, have any hobbies or interests?

- Why do they want to be part of the community? What do they want from it and what can they offer?

You can start to tag them, either in your system or figuratively in your mind, and work out whether they are a good fit to go with the housemates. They don't have to be carbon copies of each other, because a mix of people and personalities is good, but having commonalities is definitely where you want to aim.

It's key not to mix housemate types – ie students with professionals – because they are at different life and mindset stages. Some will want to go out and party on a Tuesday night when the others have work the next morning; some will work during the day while others will work at night. Be sensitive to your existing housemates, because the last thing you want is to move one person in and have five people moving out because of them. (This has happened and is a story for another day!) A harmonious house is a happy house.

Nurture your customers

Once a new housemate moves in, they need to be introduced to the group and made to feel welcome. This is part of every co-living operator's 'handbook': the check-in or onboarding process. It should be more than just, 'Here is your room and here's how to use the shower.' Use subtle suggestions of a house meal, night out or movie night. It could even be provided by you: if it's the difference between a six-month or eighteen-month tenancy, then it's well worth it for the price of a few pizzas.

This is the beginning of the nurture process, which is essentially a role that either you or your agent, or one of their team, will take on.

USING A COMMUNITY MANAGER

We have a nationwide community manager whose role it is to check on the new housemates and ensure they have settled in OK. This person isn't on the day-to-day operational side of things, because that's a different part of the business.

Our aim is to make the operational side as efficient and effective as possible, so it requires minimal input and that the main focus of the team can be on nurturing houses and relationships. We want to ensure occupants stay a long time and are happy to continue to pay a premium rent.

Our community manager encourages the building of meaningful relationships not only within the property, but also within our wider portfolio in an area. A community can be more than within each house: it can be a region of customers. We leverage those local business connections to find spaces, and financial incentives to use their spaces.

The most effective way to nurture relationships is to overdeliver as a landlord. The housemate has bought into your brand and a vision of their life in the property. If you can surpass their expectations, the number of reasons for moving out decrease. Here are some ideas to surprise:

- Welcome pack
- Birthday or Christmas gifts
- Dinner and drinks for the house (for example, pizza and beers)
- Access to sports or movies packages on TV for a period of time
- Organised and bespoke events

We'll cover that last one in more detail next.

Gatherings are a sure-fire way to encourage the forming of meaningful relationships. The idea is that your community manager will put these on to begin with, and eventually the housemates will organise events themselves over the long term. These events could be at the house for just the housemates, or it could be across a region.

Possible events include:

- Games night
- Poker night
- Movie night
- Book club
- Watching sport
- Dinner
- Cocktail-making class, etc

The list goes on; going back to the Listen part of the Co-living Approach, ask them what they want to do. It doesn't have to cost you money, just a little effort on your part.

Gatherings cement relationships and form new ones. They also show that your brand of shared home is different. If you invest in multiple areas, your ethos can spill out and keep customers within your business. Why not even hold a national event for your brand?

Who should manage the property?

Should you use agents, or manage them yourself? The thing is, not all agents are created equal, and not all experienced letting agents know how to approach HMOs. Some claim that they can, but stumble at the first hurdle. Scott Baker Properties has changed agents before due to lack of delivery, and no doubt it won't be the last time.

Interviewing agents

The first thing you need to find out is how much they know about HMO and particularly co-living lettings. Here's our initial checklist:

- Do you specialise in HMOs?

- What percentage of your books are rooms?

- How do you view an HMO – do you find them easy or difficult to manage?

- How many rooms do you currently manage?

- How many rooms do you currently have empty?

- How long, on average, is a room on the market before it fills?

- What demographic of tenants would you recommend, based on the area?

- Will you provide references? (Always speak to another landlord on their books.)

- Will you let us view properties you're currently managing?

Consider doing a sense-check, like our fellow investor did (see Chapter 16) – send a mystery shopper, perhaps a friend or colleague, or one of your current customers to ask the agent questions and gauge how well they sell the room. Sit down with your 'informant' afterwards and ask them for feedback: it will help you assess just how good the agent is.

Self-managing

If you are close enough geographically to your properties, or you develop a large enough portfolio in one area, you might want to consider self-managing.

For example, let's say you have five HMOs with six rooms apiece, each renting monthly for £500. That's £15,000 per month. Assuming an HMO letting agent costs you 15%, their take is £1,750 per month. Could you use that money instead to pay someone to personally look after your properties for maybe an hour a week per property: ie, five hours a week? Of course! That's what comes with economies of scale.

The person you employ must be liked by your tenants, without being their friend. That's because your representative needs to be able to secure their monthly rental payments, as well as placate them when things go wrong.

Self-managing should save you money if the properties are within reasonable proximity of each other, and if you know what you're doing. If you don't, it will cost you more, as maintenance and loss of rent will catch up with you quickly.

TOP TIP

Give your product a name, regardless of whether you self-manage or use an agent.

If you name your product, your existing housemates can refer to your houses by that name – they are no longer just a room managed by an agent.

The Co-living Approach is how you get buy-in from your customers to trust you, buy from you and stay for the long term. Remember: there's nothing better than a raving customer to attract more customers.

PART SIX
THRIVE

18
Systems

The final principle on this adventure to becoming a Next Level Landlord is to thrive. Professionals know the two most important elements of running a business: they see new opportunities to grow and make the most of them, but they also ensure that their existing business doesn't flounder. Some find it much easier to plant many new trees yet forget to nurture the ones they planted last year. Without love and attention, they wither and struggle to get by – some make it, but some die.

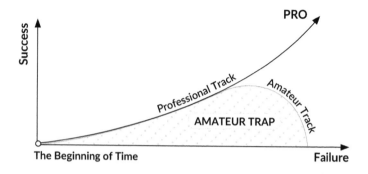

Figure 18.1: The amateur trap

I call this the 'amateur trap'. You will have every great intention to grow a successful business along the professional track, but there are four elements to be aware of to thrive:

- **Debt:** Don't let your borrowing spiral out of control. Keep your properties at a sensible loan-to-value (LTV), and a handle on the debt in your business. Increasing debt will pull you onto the amateur track. Create resilient repayment plans for any investment outside of your mortgages.

- **Evolve:** If you don't evolve as a business owner, you will definitely fall onto the amateur track. Listen to the feedback around you, and create solutions that ensure your business moves both with the times and the market.

- **Belief:** Your belief in your ability to succeed will vary from day-to-day. When it gets tough, what will bring you back to focus is a massive vision and goals that inspire you. Revisit the 'F' of the Tenant First method to create your vision.

- **Team:** The amateur track is full of people trying to do everything themselves. You must grow a great team. Most importantly, focus on their happiness and well-being, and they will focus on your business. (We've covered this in Chapter 14.)

To thrive, the solutions are to focus on your systems, ongoing sustainability, social presence and scaling your business. Let's start with systems.

There are two definitions:

1. A set of things working together as parts of a mechanism or an interconnecting network – a complex whole

2. A set of principles or procedures according to which something is done – an organised scheme or method

The first definition refers to your business when it is fully systemised. It is like the human body, which has eleven systems, each of which with their own subsystem. If we think about a business as a well-oiled machine, it has moving parts that are all managed in different departments.

What we are likely to want is a business that looks like this (Figure 18.2):

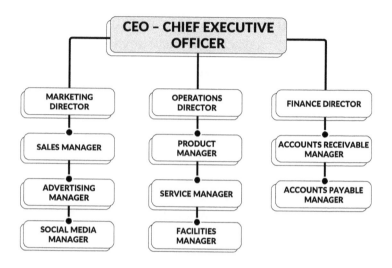

Figure 18.2: Your organisation system

This approach is covered in a great book called *The E-myth Revisited*,[33] which goes into detail on how to design what you want your end business to look like in terms of the roles within it, by working backwards.

If this diagram is your business today, ask yourself: who is doing all the roles here? Is it you, by any chance? Some of you will know these structures from being involved in companies for day-to-day jobs that you have or used to have. The same approach must be applied to your business to thrive.

---

33 M Gerber, *The E-myth Revisited: Why small businesses don't work, and what to do about it* (Harper Business, 2001)

To get there, let's look at the second definition – 'a set of principles or procedures according to which something is done' – and break it down.

To create the principles to organise your business, apply the Three Es:

1. Effective – achieves the desired outcome

2. Efficient – saves the user time and/or money

3. Easy – teachable and foolproof

There are numerous examples of how you can over-engineer a solution, such as the coffee mug that tells you how hot it is, or the Bluetooth toothbrush that I bought last year with a display that has a happy or sad face depending on my competency as a brusher. (The display is firmly in the drawer still.)

The Three Es is a test by which to run your systems as you create and implement them. If a system isn't all three of the above, ditch it and start again.

To begin to systemise, use the Three Ts method:

1. **Track:** Track everything that you do in the running of the business for a week (or at least one day). Use

a time tracking app to see how much of your time you use for various tasks, then divide these into categories: high-value, mid-value and low-value. Learn to outsource all but the high-value tasks, and as you do outsource, ask yourself this question: could this task be automated?

2. **Transcribe:** Record everything you do as you do it and create a manual. Not a 1,000-page tome; a reference of explainer videos is all you need. Just do it once, record yourself explaining the task, and add it to your shared database.

3. **Teach:** Share it with your team: they will give you the best feedback as to whether your system meets the Three Es test.

Systemising is about removing yourself from most of the elements of your business. You can do this either with staff or technology, but do bear in mind that technology is only as good as the people who set it up and use it. It's a tool and should not be confused with a system itself.

Incomes and outgoings

Systemise these to ensure you get paid and don't overpay for anything. Have systems to track everything: late rent payments, arrears, empty rooms and creeping expenses dent your bottom line, so track everything.

MONITOR YOUR AGENTS

Not all agents do their job perfectly in every area, including reporting to you. Maintain your own spreadsheet to track expected income versus what is received.

Some agents will provide an arrears report while others only report on rents received, without you realising you're missing a few hundred pounds here or there.

A spreadsheet also helps you easily track any arrears. All tenants intend to pay on time but some forget: some might pay weekly or monthly.

Maintenance

Run a common-sense check on maintenance to avoid unnecessary charges. Ensure that your agent checks first over the phone, before sending out a maintenance person who may charge a callout fee.

Energy usage

This is a potentially flexible expense. Once you own a few properties, you have some negotiating power. Speak to energy companies and request quotes; there are energy comparison sites that will do this for you too.

Once you've got a good-value rate, it's time to track the usage of each house, something that gets easier over time. When starting out you won't have an idea how much each house is going to cost energy-wise; but later on, you can gauge how much energy costs are per month versus how much they should or could be.

TOP TIP

What is tracked and measured can be managed. Set your desired key performance indicators, and test against them.

Additionally, if you habitually track this in a spreadsheet of usage and costs, you'll be the first to know when one of your tenants sets up a 'farming business' in their room (or these days, a crypto-mining rig). Using smart meters and smart Wi-Fi-enabled thermostats are great tools to aid you in this system.

USE A TRACKING TOOL

My favourite system for managing and tracking these items is COHO. As previously mentioned in Chapter 15, this HMO and co-living management tool has the goal to be able to automate the whole management process, if the user chooses. Agents can use it as well as the landlord.

We use it to manage most of our stock, but also to manage managers and track income and outgoings. If your agent is using a system, you as landlord will always want to be able to access the data on your terms. COHO allows for this.

Staff

Once we have thought about the roles and the auto-mated systems that you can use in your business, we need people to fill those roles. Always start with the finance side first – tracking the money is so important.

Bookkeeper

A bookkeeper is your ideal first hire: someone well versed in cloud-based accounting software, with UK property knowledge. They don't have to be full-time – one day per month may be fine to begin with; they can grow with your business.

Administrator

The next person is someone to help with your day-to-day operation: administration and property man-agement. They could be anywhere in the world. We use virtual assistants (VAs), and have team members based in the UK, Philippines and the Middle East.

I recommend using a specialist recruitment consultant for VAs and use their expertise at filtering applicants. (Most of the horror stories I hear about outsourcing to other countries comes when people go into hiring cold.)

Personal assistance

Finally, systemise your personal life. Get people to help you free up time to focus on those high-income tasks: it could be a cleaner, gardener, even a cook. Your hourly/day rate is a lot more than you think it is, especially if you have grand plans:

$$\text{Ideal Day Rate} = \frac{\text{Goal Annual Income}}{\text{Goal Number of Working Days}}$$

Let's say that your goal annual income is £250,000, and you want to work half of the year. Assuming 261 working days per year, that's a goal of approximately 130 working days:

$$\frac{£250,000 \text{ Goal Annual Income}}{130 \text{ days}} = £1,923 \text{ per day}$$

Prioritise personal development

When you free up your time, remember to prioritise your own personal development. Reading or listening to books, like this one, will give you great ideas and keep you in a positive state of mind to help combat when the negative thoughts creep in.

Do you have a system for your personal development? An easy one is to have a reading list for each year. I suggest at least one per month, if not two. Of course, thank you for picking this one up, but don't stop here!

19
Sustainable

In today's world, sustainability is at the forefront of most people's minds – but most don't know how to be or become more sustainable, so they do the bare minimum with what they can control. Maybe sorting the recycling at home or ensuring it's clean before it goes in the bin.

In our property business there are three elements that we can focus on for sustainability: utilities, the build process and furnishings.

Utilities

From a purely financial aspect, it makes sense to aim to save energy and therefore cost in our properties.

But it also helps our wider responsibilities as a Next Level Landlord to have a conscience and awareness of the wider impact of our business on local, national and international communities.

Green energy

How can we act responsibly? First, by choosing a supplier that only uses green, sustainable or renewable energy sources. But how about creating our own energy at the property? There are government incentives to install energy-generating systems such as solar panels and heat pumps. They won't be relevant to every property, but we can always ask ourselves the question: can we implement solar or an air-source heat pump? Ground source is also on the radar, but we need much larger grounds than some of our properties.

As technology improves in these sectors and become more cost-effective, we will be looking to implement this more – and I suggest you do the same. One of our goals at Scott Baker Properties is to have a completely self-sufficient HMO energy-wise. It reduces our expenses over the long term and is a big selling point to the younger generations living in shared accommodation who are aware of their own environmental impact.

Usage

About usage in the home: this covers electricity, gas and water. Some housemates are environmentally conscious, while others are not. Some will take advantage of the 'bills-included' nature of the rent, take 20-minute-long showers and leave the heating on. Smart thermostats can help you to control this; but fundamentally, if you can educate your tenants to be more aware, they can self-regulate their usage.

As well as smart thermostats with sensible programmes that you can control and temperature boosts that the housemates can control, you can install sensors for lighting to turn them off when there's nobody around, and water-saving measures such as taps that mix air into the flow to reduce the amount of water, but not the perceived pressure.

Economical appliances are important too: we always provide a dishwasher and encourage it to be used on 'eco mode' when full.

Our approach is to include this aspect as part of the new housemate's induction. We tell them that the house is an environmentally conscious house, that all the other tenants are aware of this and act responsibly. This, along with well-positioned subtle reminders in the house to recycle, save water and energy, generally yields results.

The build process

This is a tricky one, because the construction industry isn't quite there with cost-effective eco-build methods yet. The new-build sector is ahead here, because houses can be prefabricated off-site and assembled, which dramatically reduces waste and CO_2 emissions.

When we are doing conversions, there may be some elements that can be prefabricated, but it is more likely that our teams will be constructing on-site. Using wood from sustainable sources is one way to make an impact, as well as ensuring you are insulating the property well in walls, roof and windows. This will dramatically reduce bills and keep housemates happier.

Furnishings

When choosing furnishings, consider the environment. For example, as landlords, it's important to use durable furniture that is timeless in design and of eco-friendly material, including buying from vintage interior and charity shops, and places that source second-hand furniture of high quality: eg eBay and vinterior.co.

If you are doing this project by yourself and have time to spend on this, visiting charity shops or sourcing second-hand furniture online that fits your interior style is a good option. If your time and resources are limited, you may need to give pieces a facelift, replacing handles, sanding, refinishing or painting. Always ensure that second-hand furniture is properly treated to be fire retardant.

Durable furniture can also be built-in, which encourages a long life. We are exploring working with a furniture designer who uses wood from a sustainable forest who will recycle or repair any furniture that becomes damaged.

As Next Level Landlords we are already taking the long view by investing in our properties, wanting them to perform and ensuring that the product and service are as good in 20 years as they are today. With that in mind, it makes sense to think about running costs, and how long what we create and provide will last.

20
Socialising And Scaling

As I've outlined in this book, you will thrive much more by working with others than by attempting to work alone. I know this – all of my businesses are joint ventures. I perform better when working with others, and generally this will be true of all businesses. Even if the business has a figurehead, success is down to a combination of skills brought by others.

TOP TIP

Only work with those whom you know, like and trust.

If you have those people in place now, you are heading in the right direction; if you can't find them, this chapter is about putting yourself out there to attract what you need for your business, by being sociable and networking – whether in-person or virtually.

One thing that the current Covid-19 pandemic has taught us is that 'in-person' no longer needs to be in the same room. People can get the same value and connection with others, if not more, through technology. Niall and I even set up a new joint venture throughout the 2020 lockdown, which will lead to the improvement of shared-living management (thecohome.life). We hadn't even met the guys involved in-person before incorporating, just via Zoom meetings.

Everything is online and offline these days: it's all about how people perceive that connection with others. This gives us the opportunity to network locally, nationally and globally.

Social media

Getting online is the easiest and best way to start new relationships. If you already do a lot of this, you'll probably find making connections and raising finance easier than most, because more people know who you are. This is what online networking does: it raises your personal profile. More people listen to what you have to say, and they approach you.

If you're new to social media, or perhaps you're on there seeing lots of property posts and wishing you had the time and the energy to post, let's think about your options. You may be comfortable with Facebook, but haven't a clue about Instagram. Twitter might be your bag, but LinkedIn is totally foreign to you. Have you even heard of TikTok, or Clubhouse?

If you are not sure where to post, pick a channel and stick to it, particularly if you're already comfortable with it. Apply yourself to master it alone; don't worry about doing multiple posts across multiple platforms. Post as often as you are comfortable with – if it's once a day, fine; if it's once a week, that's fine too. Just be consistent. Eventually, I suggest you post every day to stay on people's radar.

What content should you post about? The topic doesn't matter so much, as long as you provide value and ensure it's not all about your business – people see through that straight away. Instead, focus on how you can help others. Once you do this, your following will massively increase.

Networking

Whenever you network at an event, especially if you are attending in person, consider your goal. Is it:

- To collect as many business cards as possible?
- To speak to as many people as possible?

- To learn from the presenters?

Your intent should be to set a meet-up or a coffee/ beer goal. How many one-to-one meet-ups can you arrange after that event?

If your goal is three one-to-one meet-ups, you are likely to need ten business cards, because the others either won't have the time or may not even respond to you. To get ten cards from people you want to speak to, your aim is likely to be twenty people.

TOP TIP

Don't put your email address on your card, just your phone number and a photo – then they have to call you to catch up.

Alternatively, don't have a card: just collect them and you have control to follow up.

A three-hour networking event with two speakers of 45 minutes each leaves you 90 minutes to network, if you arrive early and stay a little late:

$$90 \text{ minutes} \div 20 \text{ people} = 4.5 \text{ minutes per person}$$

Now you must learn how to gracefully move on from a conversation after just four minutes.

Once the business is running smoothly with the systems in place that you need right now, you can think about scaling up your business to the next level.

The areas to scale up are strategy and finance.

Strategy

You can implement the Next Level HMO® strategy into the scaling of your business, but if you are going to add a lot of properties to your books, it's best to consider the impact of this.

Think back to the elements of Insight – is there enough demand for what you are planning? To scale effectively, these are the approaches you can take:

Identify commonalities

Buy houses and commercial buildings and create Next Level HMOs as described in this book, creating a brand that is unique to the market and properties that are unique to each other.

To scale quickly, it is a good idea to identify the commonalities between each project that can be repeated and systemised without losing uniqueness. For example, if there's a layout that you find that works in a lot of property types, that could be the common theme saving you time and money on each project – just repeat the space layout. If it's the light fittings that are the same, purchase a bulk order to save on cost.

Don't carbon copy each deal – use your team to give each project its identity.

Buy underperforming HMOs and add value

Buy existing HMOs that are not performing well, where you can add value through space and increasing the turnover of the property. This means that you are not adding rooms to the area, and there is a history of running the property as an HMO for planning purposes. For example, a four-bed C4 HMO in an Article 4 area could become a six-bed.

Spread your risk across multiple towns

Take a measured view and a 'team-first' approach. Get the team in place before you buy: build and lettings. Also, become good in one town first, then spread.

Going for larger markets is a safer bet, because your impact is lower when creating 100 rooms in Next Level HMOs. The smaller the market, the more impact you will make, meaning that you can quickly become your own competition. Choose your starting point, check if it works, then go hard in that area until it doesn't make sense to do more.

On the flip side, when scaling effectively, it is important to take stock and review where you're going. It can be easy to veer off-course and get caught up in the day-to-day. Someone needs to be the captain of the ship and ensure that the business stays the course, because the slightest of detours early on can take you way off-track.

Finance

Once you've got your strategy sorted, you know what institutional funding you need, but how do you fund the rest? You may well be reading this because you have some funds lined up for projects – whether your own, your business's or your life partner's. To operate at scale, you may need to leverage further, so scaling up your private finance is one on which to focus.

Raising private finance

Working with investors is how we scale up the finance side of the business. We have built our business purely on this model, which has been one of our key foci, so we have an understanding of how to approach people and who investors probably are.

There are five steps to successfully raise private finance, whether you're already doing this, or still struggling to grasp why someone would ever hand you their hard-earned cash:

1. The investment proposal

2. Distribution

3. Pitching

4. Networking

5. The follow-up

Step 1: The investment proposal

It is critical to have a proposal always ready to go, as you never know whom you might meet or when. This detailed deal appraisal will include a lot of detail about you, your experience and team, the project and plans, the numbers, and some of the information that you have researched as part of the Insight principle of this method. This is what you will print, bind and physically hand to people who express an interest.

Step 2: Distribution

There are rules governing raising finance from private investors, and what you can and can't say or do. The first thing to note is that joint ventures where there is a profit share agreement are regulated, and you are not legally permitted to advertise them.[34]

---

34 *Restrictions on the Retail Distribution of Unregulated Collective Investment Schemes and Close Substitutes: Feedback to CP12/19 including final rules* (FCA, 2013), www.fca.org.uk/publication/policy/ps13-03.pdf, accessed 19 November 2020

You can only sell these investments to high-net-worth individuals or those who can be classified as 'sophisticated investors'. These definitions appear in the *Financial Conduct Authority Handbook*, under section 4.12, 'Restrictions on the promotion of non-mainstream pooled investments'.[35]

TOP TIP

Always include a disclaimer to cover for Financial Conduct Authority requirements, and include it as a footer on every page:

'This is a document for distribution to friends and family, and is issued to high-net-worth or sophisticated investors only. It is not for public promotion and is not to be regarded as an FCA-approved regulated investment. We maintain a log of anyone who has been invited to read this document.'

The people most likely to invest with you now are those who already know you. You've undoubtedly heard the term 'six degrees of separation', whereby we are only six people away from anyone else on the planet. I call raising finance the 'six degrees of wealth creation' (Figure 21.1) – you are less than six people away from everyone who can help you to grow your business, including the money!

---

35 'Restrictions on the promotion of non-mainstream investments', *FCA Handbook* (2014), www.handbook.fca.org.uk/handbook/COBS/4/12.html, accessed 19 November 2020

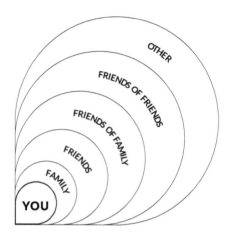

Figure 21.1: Six degrees of wealth creation

Within these 'six degrees' will be high-net-worth and sophisticated investors – you probably just don't know it yet. Start the conversation today, so that you can raise finance tomorrow.

TOP TIP

Never make assumptions about who has and doesn't have money.

Some of these relationships may take some time and cultivation before they are willing to invest. But it will be worth the effort, because they are likely to invest for a long time, and at a lower interest rate than you might anticipate.

Step 3: Pitching

When you meet people for the first time, you want to capture what you do succinctly. Some people call this an elevator or 60-second pitch. Certain networking events grant you 30–60 seconds to pitch to the room. That's quite a challenge!

What do you say? Here are some pointers. Jot down your answers to start piecing your pitch together.

- Who are you? Be personable, distinctive, memorable. What makes you unique?

- What is your mission, your vision? Get others to buy into who you are and what you stand for, eg, 'I'm creating 100 rooms this year to help increase the standard of shared accommodation in [town].'

- Why are you talking to them? You can't pitch for money directly, due to the Financial Conduct Authority reasons that we have already discussed, but you are permitted to say that you're there to meet people who can get involved in your business.

- How you intend to help others – it's a turn-off when it's all about you. Focus on what you offer people in return. 'I have expert knowledge and contacts in [their area] and I can find properties for people who are looking.'

Be confident – even if you mess up, when you present with confidence, someone will be intrigued. Don't memorise your speech! It's fine to write out your initial draft and refine it until you're happy with it, but it needs to sound natural, not forced. Use bullet points on an index card that you keep handy, and practise going through them until it becomes second nature.

Step 4: Networking

Follow the tips set out in the 'Social' part of this method and remember to have a strategy in place when you network. Don't just go for a jolly!

Step 5: The follow-up

The deal is always done in the follow-up. If you're not doing this, you're missing hundreds of opportunities. If you're out networking a lot, you need to keep track of all of the people you meet and agree to catch up with afterwards. Create a system to track this, whether a list on your wall, spreadsheet or customer relationship management programme.

When following up with a potential investor, never rush them. Give them time to consider, but go for clarity: 'Are you ready to go for this deal?' 'Are you going to invest?' What you want is a 'yes', 'no' or 'not now'. If you have that, you can move forward. If they prevaricate and keep repeating 'maybe', they're likely to be a 'no'.

TOP TIP

Always aim to meet your investor in-person or by video conferencing. Most communication is non-verbal: if you can see each other's faces, you'll develop a stronger bond, which can lead to quicker or more certain investment.

Systemise everything. Ultimately, you want to be able to take yourself out of the business and still have it operate. We are all looking for more time and financial freedom.

Look for sustainable solutions. Ensure you have impact, however small, on leaving future generations with a better world.

Grow your own personal profile through social media and networking. Becoming a perceived success breeds more success. I'm not suggesting fake it until you make it, but being known in your industry will always bring opportunity your way.

Scale and scale well. The key is to stay true to your core mission, vision and values. If you do that as a Next Level Landlord, success is inevitable.

Conclusion

By now, either you'll have complete clarity on what to do, and the excitement to move forwards as a Next Level Landlord, or you might be overwhelmed by how different the five principles are from where you thought you were going as a co-living landlord.

It's true that this is not an easy road, for the faint-hearted or the amateur investor. If it was, everyone would do it. You've been reading this book because you're ready to make a change to how you operate, or you have just started out and want to get it right from the outset. It is the beginnings of a business and change that takes time and effort. That's why it's important to know what you're getting into, before you begin. Rest assured: with enough time and effort, once your business gets moving, it's highly rewarding.

Either way, we have busted some myths along the way to get you thinking differently about this industry. Co-living is not just another name for HMO, it's a way of being. The HMO is the physical thing that you create, but co-living is the sense of community within a property. It's the magic sauce that gives your business real legs.

The HMO market is too busy for me

If you're still thinking 'the HMO market is saturated, this isn't for me', remember that a Next Level HMO® is not the same product as everyone else's. It has those three fundamental differences: quality design, space and service.

By creating these within your property and pitching it in the top 5% of your market, *you* take the tenants, not someone else. Your product is the one that stands out.

Every other investor is doing this

Is everyone doing this? This is a misconception: not everyone is doing HMOs. A lot of people are scared of them – that's good, they should be. A lot of people think they are hard – that's good, they are! And they're getting harder; but as they become harder to create in planning terms and to license, fewer people will be attracted to this strategy. That is still good, because demand for quality is increasing. There is a shift happening right now – a tipping point – where the old landlord will disappear quietly and sell off, and the Next Level Landlord will come in and thrive.

Which side do you want to be on?

I don't have the time or money

What if you have got to the end of this book and realised you don't have the capital to do this strategy? No doubt someone else is reading this book who does have the capital but thinking they don't have the time to jump into this.

Time is all down to priorities. Is cultivating your business a priority for you? If so, you will find the time to make this work: one solution is to find that buddy or future joint venture partner from a network of like-minded people.

To help, I've put together a business diagnostic tool which asks some simple questions about your existing business. It scores on the different principles, to see how close you are to being a Next Level Landlord: www.thehmoplatform.co.uk / takethequiz.

Back in the chapter on strategy and vision, we examined what we call the keys to continued growth: what's required in learning to become motivated

(Figure 22.1). Hopefully what this book endeavours to provide will motivate you to begin the journey, building momentum as you gain experience.

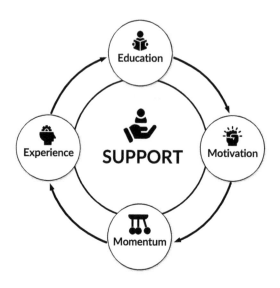

Figure 22.1: Keys to continued growth

Building momentum takes a lot of effort. Think of it like driving an old steam train: it takes a lot of fuel to get started. You have to light the fire, and get the water up to temperature before it can begin to move. Keep throwing fuel on to keep the fire burning hot, as you gain speed. The train then generates its own momentum, and the fire only needs small, albeit regular, top-ups. Education is the accelerant that initially fuels your fire, followed by your environment, the company you keep and your support network – which all provide the top-ups to keep you moving forward.

If we could keep focused 100% of the time, this would be easier, but it's not human nature to be able do this. Life gets in the way: we get distracted, and when we get momentarily derailed, we beat ourselves up for it. We need periodic reminders outside of ourselves to keep us on track. I call this the focus trajectory (Figure 22.2).

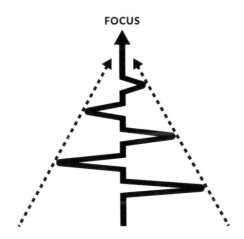

Figure 22.2: The focus trajectory

By having regular touchpoints, you increase the amount of time you remain focused – when you're 'in the zone' – which reduces the length of time you spend unfocused. The more you install these reminders and support networks around you, the more likely you are to succeed on this route you've chosen.

Thank you for choosing to read this book to be one of those touchpoints, and for taking one more step along the road to becoming a successful Next Level Landlord.

The world needs more people like you.

Acknowledgements

Thank you to Andi Cooke, Lloyd Girardi and Jon McDermott for being the catalyst for writing this book. It has been on the cards for a couple of years, but never came to anything. I said so many times, 'I should do it' – but in Bali 2019 we set the goal to ensure I did, and here it is. The whole book-writing process was made a lot easier with the help of Siobhan, who had the unenviable task of cutting my first draft in half; Ricardo, for the wonderful graphics; and of course, the team at Rethink for focusing me to get it done. Thanks also to the team at The Collective for sharing their insights into co-living, which have added tremendous value to the book.

To my parents, Sarah and Peter, for braving the beginning of this property adventure together, and raising me of course – thank you. Similarly, to Niall, my business partner and best of friends, for keeping me on the straight and narrow: letting me run with an idea but then telling me 'no' when it's needed! I couldn't do this without you, buddy.

Finally, thank you to my beautiful Lara for her support and patience in allowing me the space to think and write this book, and for all the other crazy ideas that I have. You are the glue that holds me together and ensures that I finish things!

The Author

Co-founder of both Scott Baker Properties and The HMO Platform, Matt is a specialist in Next Level HMO® and co-living developments. He is recognised in the property industry as one of the country's leading HMO developers and was the UK's first co-living educator.

Starting life as a musician, Matt has always had a creative side, composing and performing as a pianist in numerous collaborations. He also grew and sold a successful musical education business. Matt aims to create meaningful relationships within his property development and training businesses.

His customer-first approach led to the successful creation of a £5 million property portfolio in his first four years of investment, using mostly investor finance.

Matt's wider vision is to have a positive impact on shared-living communities across the globe, to create lifelong peace of mind and well-being for both tenant and landlord.

Contact

You can learn more about Matt's developments at www.scottbakerproperties.co.uk.

Learn more about how Matt educates, coaches and develops co-living landlords and developers at www. thehmoplatform.co.uk.

See the Co-living Approach in action through Matt's co-living management business at thecohome.life.

Connect with Matt on social media: @clearlymattbaker.

Lightning Source UK Ltd.
Milton Keynes UK
UKHW021600110621
385347UK00001B/1